CONTENTS

Brazil's captain Dunga lift[s]

© 1998 Grandreams Ltd

Written by Rob Holden
Designed by Jeremy Paxton

Published by
Grandreams Ltd
435-437 Edgware Road
Little Venice
London W2 1TH

Printed in Belgium

£4.99

THE BIGGEST WORLD CUP FINALS *Ever!*

THE SIXTEENTH WORLD CUP FINALS WILL be staged in France this summer. No less than 32 nations will battle it out for the honour of being crowned World Champions of Football – that's eight more than in the 1994 finals in the United States. This makes this year's contest the BIGGEST World Cup finals in the entire history of the tournament.

The schedule of 64 top class matches will be played out at ten venues across France – from Lens in the north to Marseille in the south. Nine of these super stadia have been spruced up for the occasion, in a programme of redevelopment and refurbishment spread over many months.

The drama will start with TWO Opening Ceremonies: the first, on 9 June, will be a parade through the streets of Paris ending at the Place de la Concorde. The second ceremony will take place in the brand new

We've made it! Cameroon (left), Morocco (above)

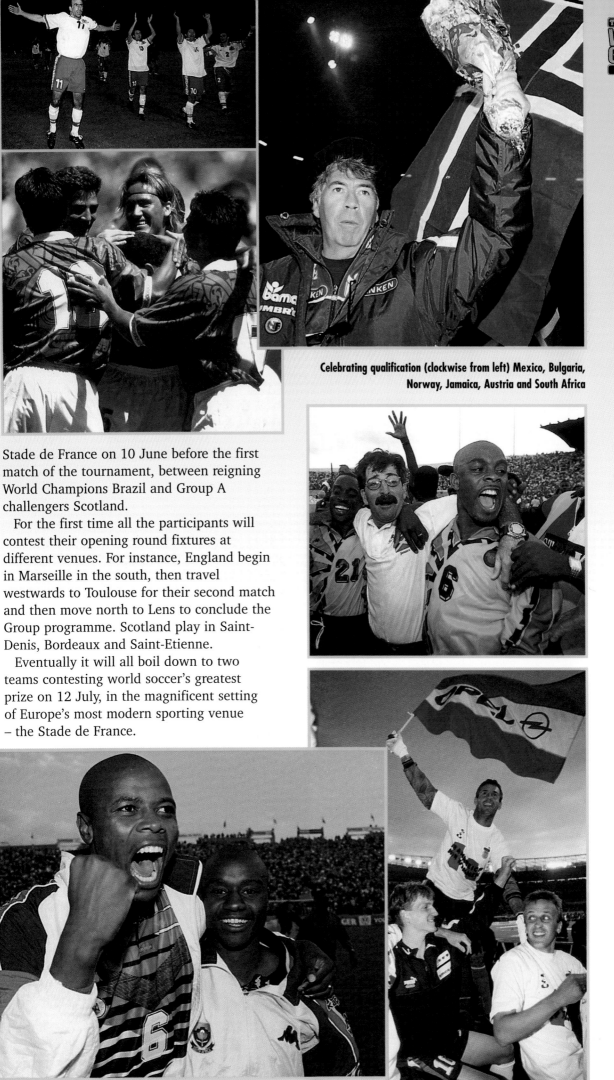

Celebrating qualification (clockwise from left) Mexico, Bulgaria, Norway, Jamaica, Austria and South Africa

Stade de France on 10 June before the first match of the tournament, between reigning World Champions Brazil and Group A challengers Scotland.

For the first time all the participants will contest their opening round fixtures at different venues. For instance, England begin in Marseille in the south, then travel westwards to Toulouse for their second match and then move north to Lens to conclude the Group programme. Scotland play in Saint-Denis, Bordeaux and Saint-Etienne.

Eventually it will all boil down to two teams contesting world soccer's greatest prize on 12 July, in the magnificent setting of Europe's most modern sporting venue – the Stade de France.

STADE DE FRANCE - SAINT DENIS — CAPACITY 80,000

The 1998 World Cup final will be played in this brand new state-of-the-art super stadium. This wonderful venue will also stage the Opening Ceremony, the opening match (Brazil v Scotland), four more opening round Group matches, one second round match, a quarter-final encounter and a semi-final. The Stade de France is situated in Saint-Denis which lies to the north of Paris.

PARC DES PRINCE - PARIS — CAPACITY 49,500

This famous venue is home to soccer clubs Paris Saint-Germain and Racing de Paris. The Parc will stage four opening group games, one second round match and the third place play-off.

STADE DE LA BEAUJOIRE - NANTES — CAPACITY 40,000

The Stade de la Beaujoire is home to FC Nantes Atlantique, and will stage five opening group games (including Brazil v Morocco) and a quarter-final match.

PARC LESCURE - BORDEAUX — CAPACITY 36,500

The Parc Lescure will stage five opening group games (including Scotland v Norway) and one second round fixture. This stadium is home to Les Girondins de Bordeaux.

MUNICIPAL STADIUM - TOULOUSE — CAPACITY 37,000

The Municipal Stadium, home of Toulouse FC, will stage five opening group games (including Romania v England) and a second round match.

THE VEN

STADE FELIX BOLLAERT - LENS — CAPACITY 42,000

The northernmost outpost of the World Cup finals. The Félix Bollaert Stadium will stage five group matches (including Colombia v England) and a second round match. This stadium is home to Racing Club du Lens.

STADE DE GERLAND - LYON — CAPACITY 45,000

The Stade de Gerland, home of Olympique Lyonnais, will stage five opening group matches (including France v Denmark) and one of the quarter-finals.

STADE GEOFFROY-GUICHARD - ST. ETIENNE — CAPACITY 36,000

The Geoffroy-Guichard Stadium is home to Saint-Etienne, one of France's most successful clubs. Five group games (including Scotland v Morocco) and a second round match will take place here.

STADE VELODROME - MARSEILLE — CAPACITY 60,000

The southernmost outpost of the World Cup finals, and home to Olympique Marseille. The World Cup draw was held in the Velodrome which will also stage four group matches (including England's opener against Tunisia), a second round game, a quarter-final and a semi-final.

STADE DE LA MOSSON - MONTPELLIER — CAPACITY 36,500

The Stade de la Mosson is home to the Montpellier Herault Sports Club. Five group games and a second round match will be played here.

TURN TO PAGE 60 FOR MATCH DETAILS AND YOUR FABULOUS WORLD CUP FINALS COUNTDOWN CHART

TOTALLY 100%
WORLD CUP 98
UNOFFICIAL

WORLD CUP FINALS 1998
– The DRAW

REIGNING CHAMPIONS BRAZIL AND HOST nation France were automatically seeded for the Group stage of the 1998 World Cup finals. Under a system based on the current World Rankings list and performances in the last three World Cups Germany, Spain, Italy, Argentina, Romania and Holland were also seeded. The most notable absentee from this list was England, whose failure to qualify for the 1994 World Cup finals now contributed to their 'second string' status in 1998.

On 4 December 1997, before the draw took place in the Marseille Velodrome, millions of TV viewers tuned-in to watch a Gala Match between Europe and the Rest of the World. The two squads were made up of players representing all 32 of the World Cup qualifying nations.

After the match FIFA General Secretary Sepp Blatter, assisted by some great stars of the past, conducted the draw with his usual style and good humour. At the end of this elaborate ceremony each of the eight seeded teams were joined by their Group opponents...

GROUP A
BRAZIL
Scotland
Morocco
Norway

GROUP B
ITALY
Chile
Cameroon
Austria

GROUP C
FRANCE
South Africa
Saudi Arabia
Denmark

GROUP D
SPAIN
Nigeria
Paraguay
Bulgaria

GROUP E
HOLLAND
Belgium
South Korea
Mexico

GROUP F
GERMANY
USA
Yugoslavia
Iran

GROUP G
ROMANIA
Colombia
England
Tunisia

GROUP H
ARGENTINA
Japan
Jamaica
Croatia

The Grand Draw takes place in Marseille

8

ALL-STAR GALA MATCH

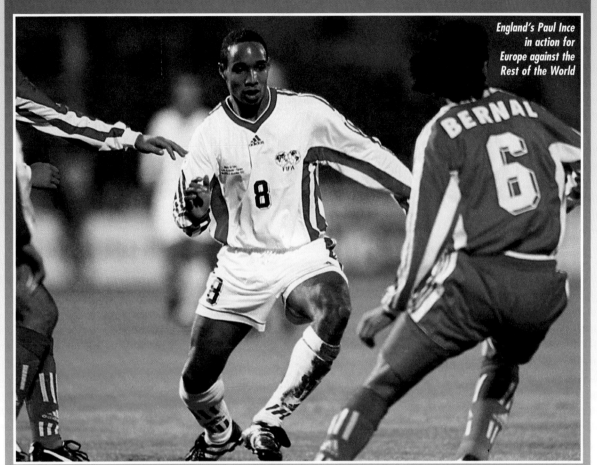

England's Paul Ince in action for Europe against the Rest of the World

EUROPE 2 - REST OF THE WORLD 5
Marseille Velodrome, Attendance: 37,050

Europe were first on the scoresheet, when Marius Lacatus seized on a defensive error to score a simple goal in the opening minute. But 'The Rest', inspired by man-of-the-match Ronaldo, soon took charge to win with a 5-2 margin. Paul Ince represented England, but it was another Premiership player, Deon Burton of Derby County, who enjoyed perhaps the proudest moment of the match when he ran on as a second-half sub for Ronaldo.

EUROPE – Kopke (Germany); Pfeifenberger (Austria), Hierro (Spain), Costacurta (Italy), Lemoine (Belgium), Lacatus (Romania), Balakov (Bulgaria), Ince (England), Zidane (France, capt), Boksic (Croatia), Kluivert (Holland)
Subs: Grodas (Norway) for Kopke, Durie (Scotland) for Kluivert, Jokanovic (Yugoslavia) for Hierro, Colding (Denmark) for Lemoine
Scorers: Lacatus 1, Zidane 64

REST OF THE WORLD – Songo'o (Cameroon); Hong Myung-Bo (S Korea), Margas (Chile), Naybet (Morocco), Nyathi (S Africa), Nakata (Japan), Bernal (Mexico), Sellimi (Tunisia), De Avila (Colombia), Batistuta (Argentina), Ronaldo (Brazil, capt)
Subs: Rui Diaz (Paraguay) for Songo'o, Sulimani (S Arabia) for Batistuta, Wynalda (USA) for De Avila, Burton (Jamaica) for Ronaldo
Scorers: De Avila 10, Ronaldo 23, 43, Batistuta 27, 37

BRAZIL

GROUP A

THE FAVOURITE NATION OF EVERY 'neutral' football fan and a guaranteed 'full house' wherever they play. Brazil are the current World Cup holders and have won the competition a record four times. They also have the distinction of being the only country to have played in the finals stages of all fifteen World Cup competitions to date.

Brazil hosted the first World Cup finals after the Second World War and achieved their best finish up to that time, as runners-up to Uruguay. In 1954 Brazil made it to the quarter-finals in Switzerland. Then came the 1958 finals in Sweden and the start of Brazil's Golden Era. They dazzled with the fantastic skills of Garrincha, Didi, Vava and a wonderful 17-year-old player called Pelé. This youngster epitomised all of Brazil's flair and style and he scored one of the World Cup's best ever goals in the 5-2 final victory over Sweden.

Brazil won the next World Cup tournament, in Chile in 1962, beating Czechoslovakia 3-1 in the final in Santiago. In 1970, in Mexico, they won the trophy for the third time, beating

Ronaldo, arguably the best footballer in the world

Romario

BRAZIL

Italy 4-1, with arguably the finest footballing side of all time.

Twenty-four years passed before Brazil reached the World Cup final again. In 1994 the likes of Aldair, Romario, Dunga and Bebeto battled through to meet Italy in the USA. That match was deadlocked after extra-time and for the first time a World Cup final was decided with a penalty shoot-out. Brazil kept their nerve, Italy cracked.

The current Brazilian side is every bit as skilful and entertaining as its illustrious predecessors – especially in attack. New stars such as Ronaldo, Denilson (soon to become the world's most expensive player), Edmundo, and Emerson have come to the fore under coach Mario Zagallo. They will all be anxious to consolidate Brazil's reputation as 'The World Cup Specialists' and lift the game's most prestigious title for the fifth time.

Denilson

Roberto Carlos

ROUTE TO FRANCE

Automatic qualification as World Cup holders

BRAZIL FACT FILE

Colours: Yellow shirts, blue shorts, white socks
Coach: Mario Zagallo

WORLD CUP FINALS RECORD

Year	Result	Year	Result
1930	1st round	1966	1st round
1934	1st round	1970	**WORLD CHAMPIONS**
1938	3rd place	1974	4th place
1950	runners-up	1978	3rd place
1954	quarter-finalists	1982	2nd round
1958	**WORLD CHAMPIONS**	1986	quarter-finalists
1962	**WORLD CHAMPIONS**	1990	2nd round
		1994	**WORLD CHAMPIONS**

SCOTLAND

WORLD 37th RANKING

WHATEVER THE RESULT OF THEIR opening game against Brazil, Scotland will know the size of the task ahead of them, if they are to finish in first or second place in Group A. If that does happen, Scotland will have gone further in 1998 than they have in any previous World Cup finals appearance. You can be sure that Norway and Morocco will both face them with trepidation.

In qualifying for this year's finals, Scotland were in Group Four along with Austria and Sweden who were both expected to go through; also in contention were Belarus, Estonia and Latvia. The Scots' campaign began with one of the toughest games on the fixture list, away to Austria in Vienna. It proved a very physical encounter, in which the referee's whistle played an almost constant tune. But the boys in the dark blue shirts were magnificent and thoroughly deserved a share of the points in the 0-0 draw.

Things got even better in Scotland's second qualifying match – away to Latvia. John Collins had the distinction of scoring his country's first goal of the 1998 World Cup campaign. It came after 18 minutes when a set-piece free-kick taken by Gary McAllister was finished off by Collins from all of 25

Kevin Gallacher – Scotland's leading scorer on the road to France

yards. The Scots' second goal of the campaign was also a long-range strike, by Darren Jackson – his first international goal.

With Hampden Park undergoing major refurbishment, the home qualifier against Sweden was played at Rangers' Ibrox Stadium. The outcome was settled by a John McGinlay goal on eight minutes. It came from a Tom Boyd pass which found McGinlay after a clever dummy by Darren Jackson had completely bamboozled the Swedish defence. This brilliant result put Scotland on top of Group Four, ahead of Sweden on goal difference.

Scotland's 'away' fixture against Estonia was played in Monaco, after the most bizarre episode of the competition. The match had originally been scheduled earlier, in Tallin, but the Estonian team had not turned up because of a dispute over the floodlights. For a while it looked as though Scotland would be awarded the 'victory' and three 'goals'. However, FIFA eventually ruled that the game should be played on neutral territory. Hence the trip to Monaco.

Although Scotland took a point from the game – a 0-0 draw – it was a poor performance in which they reverted to uninspired long-ball tactics that failed to

Craig Burley

Colin Hendry

SCOTLAND

penetrate the Estonian defence. The travelling Scottish fans showed their disappointment as their team left the field and Craig Brown later apologised for the dire display.

Things got back on track in the next game, the return fixture against Estonia, played at Kilmarnock's Rugby Park. Tom Boyd opened the scoring with his first ever goal for Scotland, a great header in the 25th minute. Estonia almost got back into the game early in the second period, but their free-kick rebounded off Jim Leighton's crossbar. The result was put beyond doubt in the 53rd minute, when Estonian defender Janek Meet turned a Boyd cross into his own goal. Craig Brown's team was now leading the Group with eleven points, ahead of Austria who had seven points and two games in hand. The next encounter brought the two teams together at Celtic's Parkhead. Man-of-the-match was Blackburn Rovers' Kevin

Andy Goram – safe hands!

Gallacher, who scored both goals in a magnificent Scottish victory. The first came on 24 minutes after a Darren Jackson solo effort had been parried by 'keeper Konsel. The ball rebounded to Jackson, who pulled it back for Gallacher to strike from six yards. Gallacher's second goal was a magnificent curling shot into the top right-hand corner of the Austrian net, in the 77th minute. This fabulous result stretched the gap between Scotland and Austria.

But there was a great deal to do before qualification was ensured. Austria still had two games in hand, as did third-placed Sweden. Scotland's next match was against the Swedes in Gothenburg's Ullevi Stadium. Inspired by Martin Dahlin and Kennet Anderssen, the home side were dominant throughout and were two-up inside 63 minutes, both goals scored by Anderssen. Kevin Gallacher pulled one back in the 84th minute, when he connected with a Craig Burley cross to head home from six yards.

The away leg against Belarus, at the Dinamo Stadium in Minsk, saw a revival of Scottish hopes. The outcome was decided early in the second half, when Darren Jackson was fouled in the penalty area. Gary McAllister made no mistake with the spot-kick – and the dream was still alive.

Aberdeen's Pittodrie Stadium staged the return with Belarus, a match originally scheduled for 6 September. But that was the

David Hopkin

SCOTLAND FACT FILE

Colours: Dark blue shirts, white shorts, red socks
Coach: Craig Brown

WORLD CUP FINALS RECORD

1930-38	did not enter	1974	1st round
1950	did not qualify	1978	1st round
1954	1st round	1982	1st round
1958	1st round	1986	1st round
1962-70	did not qualify	1990	1st round
		1994	did not qualify

15

SCOTLAND

day of the funeral of Diana, Princess of Wales, and the fixture was rescheduled for the following day. Scotland were ahead after just five minutes, when the Belarus 'keeper dropped a Gary McAllister free-kick and Kevin Gallacher pounced to knock the ball home. In the 55th minute David Hopkin scored his first international goal after Ally McCoist had cut a fine ball back from the by-line. Three minutes later Kevin Gallacher beat two defenders before adding Scotland's third.

The visitors replied in the 75th minute when Kachuro fired home from the penalty spot after Christian Dailly had fouled Lavrik. But for Belarus it was too little, too late. Twelve minutes later, David Hopkin sealed the match with a fine solo goal.

In their final Group Four match Scotland had to beat Latvia, at Parkhead, in order to secure either first or second place. They did the job in style, winning 2-0 with goals from Kevin Gallacher (on 43 minutes) and Gordon Durie (80 minutes). Meanwhile Austria had defeated Belarus 4-0 in Vienna, to secure top spot and qualification to the finals. Scotland qualified too, as the best of the European runners-up. It was a magnificent achievement which takes them to their sixth World Cup finals in the last seven campaigns. The next hurdle for the Scots is the small matter of Brazil on Wednesday 10 June.

Duncan Ferguson

Ally McCoist in action against Austria

Stuart McCall steers the ball away from Austria's Stephan Marasek

ROUTE TO FRANCE

EUROPEAN QUALIFYING GROUP FOUR
Scotland's Results

Date	Result
31.8.96	Austria 0 - Scotland 0
5.10.96	Latvia 0 - Scotland 2
10.11.96	Scotland 1 - Sweden 0
11.2.97	Estonia 0 - Scotland 0
29.3.97	Scotland 2 - Estonia 0
2.4.97	Scotland 2 - Austria 0
30.4.97	Sweden 2 - Scotland 1
8.6.97	Belarus 0 - Scotland 1
7.9.97	Scotland 4 - Belarus 1
11.10.97	Scotland 2 - Latvia 0

Final Table

	P	W	D	L	F	A	Pts
Austria	10	8	1	1	17	4	25
SCOTLAND	10	7	2	1	15	3	23
Sweden	10	7	0	3	16	9	21
Latvia	10	3	1	6	10	14	10
Estonia	10	1	1	8	4	16	4
Belarus	10	1	1	8	5	21	4

SCOTLAND QUALIFY AS THE BEST RUNNERS-UP IN THE EUROPEAN QUALIFYING GROUPS

Complete this chart when Scotland's squad is announced

1. _____
2. _____
3. _____
4. _____
5. _____
6. _____
7. _____
8. _____
9. _____
10. _____
11. _____
12. _____
13. _____
14. _____
15. _____
16. _____
17. _____
18. _____
19. _____
20. _____
21. _____
22. _____

MOROCCO

WORLD 13th RANKING

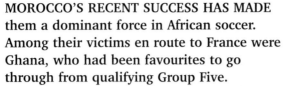

MOROCCO'S RECENT SUCCESS HAS MADE them a dominant force in African soccer. Among their victims en route to France were Ghana, who had been favourites to go through from qualifying Group Five.

Besides reaching the finals, Morocco also gave Brazil a scare in a friendly encounter last November. Morocco were clinging on for what would have been a famous 0-0 draw, but the Brazilians rallied late in the game to score twice. Nevertheless, the reigning World Champions had been shaken by the North African team. Now all Moroccan fans will be hoping that their team can go one better against the World Champions in Nantes on 16 June.

Morocco's star striker is Salaheddine Bassir, a supremely talented 25-year-old who was snapped up by Deportivo La Coruna of Spain. Another La Coruna star is defender Noureddine Naybet. And look out for Mustapha El Hadji, a midfielder who was born in France. The French wanted to cap him at Under-21 level, but he chose to play for Morocco.

The team is coached by former French international Henri Michel, who was once sacked as the French national team coach. He would no doubt love a chance for revenge.

Noureddine Naybet

Salaheddine Bassir

ROUTE TO FRANCE

AFRICA GROUP FIVE
Final Table

	P	W	D	L	F	A	Pts
MOROCCO	6	5	1	0	14	2	16
Sierra Leone	5*	2	1	2	4	6	7
Ghana	6	1	3	2	7	7	6
Gabon	5*	0	1	4	1	11	1

* Gabon v Sierra Leone postponed

MOROCCO FACT FILE

Colours: Red shirts, green shorts, red socks
Coach: Henri Michel

WORLD CUP FINALS RECORD

1930-58	did not enter	1974-82	did not qualify
1962	did not qualify	1986	2nd round
1966	did not enter	1990	did not qualify
1970	1st round	1994	1st round

NORWAY

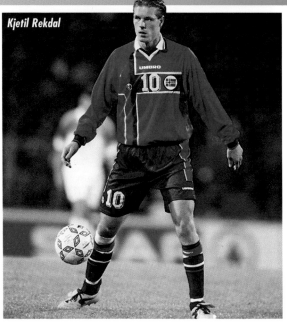

Kjetil Rekdal

WORLD 10th RANKING

NORWAY CURRENTLY PROVIDES MORE players in the English Premier League's 'foreign legion' than any other nation. Manchester United's Henning Berg, Ronny Johnsen and Ole Gunnar Solskjaer, Chelsea's Tore Andre Flo, Spurs' Frode Grodas and Liverpool's Stig Inge Bjornebye, Bjorn Kvarme and Oyvind Leonhardsen are just some of the Norwegians who strut their stuff in England.

Six victories and two draws saw Norway through European Qualifying Group Three with relative ease. Qualification was secured with a 1-0 away win in Azerbaijan, in September '97. The all-important goal came from Tore Andre Flo just before half-time.

Four days later Norway rounded off their successful campaign with a 5-0 celebratory drubbing of Switzerland in Oslo. Skipper Kjetil Rekdal was man-of-the-match, which was also notable for the return to action of the irrepressible Jahn Ivar 'Mini' Jakobsen.

Now, coach Egil Olsen will be confident that his strong defence and prolific attack will continue the momentum set up in that convincing qualification campaign. This will be Norway's third appearance in World Cup finals stages. Last time around, in 1994, they contributed to England's non-qualification woes by winning 2-0 in Oslo. Norway then went on to fall at the first hurdle in the USA.

Since then – apart from qualifying for the current World Cup finals – Norway have listed the mighty Brazil among their conquests. Last May they beat them 4-2 in Oslo, so the Brazilians will be very wary when the two teams meet in Marseille on 23 June.

EUROPEAN QUALIFYING GROUP THREE
Norway's Results

2.6.96	Norway 5 - Azerbaijan 0
9.10.96	Norway 3 - Hungary 0
10.11.96	Switzerland 0 - Norway 1
30.4.97	Norway 1 - Finland 1
8.6.97	Hungary 1 - Norway 1
20.8.97	Finland 0 - Norway 4
6.9.97	Azerbaijan 0 - Norway 1
10.9.97	Norway 5 - Switzerland 0

Final Table

	P	W	D	L	F	A	Pts
NORWAY	8	6	2	0	21	2	20
Hungary	8	3	3	2	10	8	12
Finland	8	3	2	3	11	12	11
Switzerland	8	3	1	4	11	12	10
Azerbaijan	8	1	0	7	3	22	3

Frode Grodas finds something to smile about

NORWAY FACT FILE

Colours: Red shirts, white shorts, blue socks
Coach: Egil Olsen

WORLD CUP FINALS RECORD

1930-34	did not enter	1954-90	did not qualify
1938	1st round	1994	1st round
1950	did not enter		

19

ITALY

Gianfranco Zola

THE 'AZZURRI' QUALIFIED FOR THE 1998 World Cup finals unbeaten and with just two goals conceded. Yet somehow they made heavy weather of the campaign. They began well enough, with four straight victories – including a 1-0 win against England at Wembley, settled by a Gianfranco Zola wonder goal – but three later draws slowed their progress.

In April '97 Poland, a team with a lot to prove and an outside chance of qualification, played their hearts out to hold the Italians 0-0. In the return match Italy made no mistake and beat the Poles 3-0. The next game should have boosted Italy's chances of qualification. But, as England were despatching Moldova at Wembley, Italy were once again struggling to hold on to a 0-0 scoreline against a spirited Georgian side in Tbilisi.

The Group stage came to a head with that classic red-blooded encounter against England in Rome last October. The 0-0 draw sent England through and left Italy having to face Russia in the second place play-offs.

Coach Cesare Maldini knew his side still had a fight ahead. For the first leg in Moscow, he reorganised his line-up and opted for a more physical approach. The match was played in atrocious conditions that brought out the vivid orange football which always signifies the worst of winter encounters. Italy held on for

GROUP B

Casiraghi celebrates!!

Roberto Di Matteo

Italy's captain Paolo Maldini

a 1-1 draw, their goal coming from Christian Vieri. The second leg, played in Naples, went Italy's way when Pierluigi Casiraghi scored the only goal of a grim game to take his side through to the finals.

ROUTE TO FRANCE

EUROPEAN QUALIFYING GROUP TWO
Italy's Results

5.10.96	Moldova 1 - Italy 3
9.10.96	Italy 1 - Georgia 0
12.2.97	England 0 - Italy 1
29.3.97	Italy 3 - Moldova 0
2.4.97	Poland 0 - Italy 0
30.4.97	Italy 3 - Poland 0
10.9.97	Georgia 0 - Italy 0
11.10.97	Italy 0 - England 0

Final Table

	P	W	D	L	F	A	Pts
England	8	6	1	1	15	2	19
ITALY	8	5	3	0	11	1	18
Poland	8	3	1	4	10	12	10
Georgia	8	3	1	4	7	9	10
Moldova	8	0	0	8	2	21	0

PLAY-OFFS

29.10.97	Russia 1 - Italy 1
15.11.97	Italy 1 - Russia 0

ITALY FACT FILE

Colours: Blue shirts, white shorts, blue socks
Coach: Cesare Maldini

WORLD CUP FINALS RECORD

1930	did not enter	1966	1st round
1934	**WORLD CHAMPIONS**	1970	**RUNNERS-UP**
1938	**WORLD CHAMPIONS**	1974	1st round
1950	1st round	1978	4th place
1954	1st round	1982	**WORLD CHAMPIONS**
1958	did not qualify	1986	2nd round
1962	1st round	1990	3rd place
		1994	**RUNNERS-UP**

CHILE

WORLD 7th RANKING

CHILE CLINCHED THE FOURTH QUALIFYING place in the South American 'round robin' system. This success marks their first World Cup finals appearance since 1982.

En route to France, Chile notched-up more goals than any other South American qualifier – 32. Included in that tally were a 6-0 thrashing of Venezuela, a 4-1 victory over Colombia and a 4-0 drubbing of Peru.

Star players in Chile's squad are the veteran striker Ivan Zamorano and Marcelo Salas. Zamorano was injured during the latter stages of Chile's World Cup campaign, but Salas kept the momentum going by scoring a brilliant hat-trick in the victory over Peru in Santiago, and he scored in the 3-0 win against Bolivia which ensured Chile's qualification.

Twenty-two year-old Salas is a star striker with River Plate in Argentina. But he seems destined to come to Europe and has already caught the eye of top clubs like Juventus and Manchester United. English fans saw a sample of his immense talent at Wembley in February, when he scored a wonder goal and a penalty in Chile's 2-0 victory in a friendly encounter.

ROUTE TO FRANCE

SOUTH AMERICAN ROUND ROBIN LEAGUE
Final Table (top four qualify)

	P	W	D	L	F	A	Pts
Argentina	16	8	6	2	23	13	30
Paraguay	16	9	2	5	21	14	29
Colombia	16	8	4	4	23	15	28
CHILE	16	7	4	5	32	18	25
Peru	16	7	4	5	19	20	25
Ecuador	16	6	3	7	22	21	21
Uruguay	16	6	3	7	18	21	21
Bolivia	16	4	5	7	18	21	17
Venezuela	16	0	3	13	8	41	3

Clarence Acuna

CHILE FACT FILE

Colours: Red shirts, blue shorts, white socks
Coach: Nelson Acosta

WORLD CUP FINALS RECORD

1930	1st round	1966	1st round
1934-38	did not enter	1970	did not qualify
1950	1st round	1974	1st round
1954	did not enter	1978	did not qualify
1958	did not qualify	1982	1st round
1962	3rd Place	1986-94	did not qualify

CAMEROON

WORLD 49th RANKING

CAMEROON HAVE BEEN GREAT WORLD Cup favourites ever since 1990, when they beat the then reigning World Champions Argentina in the opening game in Italy. They went on to reach the quarter-finals before going down 3-2 to England. In 1994 Cameroon again made it to the World Cup finals, but failed to progess beyond the opening group stage. This year the 'Indomitable Lions' are back again, as the first African nation to qualify for three successive World Cups.

Ironically it is this success that makes life difficult for Coach Jean Manga Onguene. Cameroon internationals have been snapped-up by clubs all over the world, which makes regular get-togethers relatively difficult. Onguene's team was hardly a settled one during qualification. Look out for eccentric 'keeper Jacques Songo'o and super-striker Patrick Mboma – and listen out for the Lions' Roar!

ROUTE TO FRANCE

AFRICA GROUP FOUR
Final Table

	P	W	D	L	F	A	Pts
CAMEROON	6	4	2	0	10	4	14
Angola	6	2	4	0	7	4	10
Zimbabwe	6	1	1	4	6	7	4
Togo	6	1	1	4	6	14	4

CAMEROON FACT FILE

Colours: Green shirts, red shorts, yellow socks
Coach: Jean Manga Onguene

WORLD CUP FINALS RECORD

1930-66	did not enter	1986	did not qualify
1970-78	did not qualify	1990	quarter-finals
1982	1st round	1994	1st round

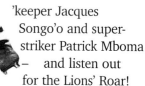
Jacques Songo'o

22

AUSTRIA

TOTALLY 100%
WORLD CUP 98
UNOFFICIAL

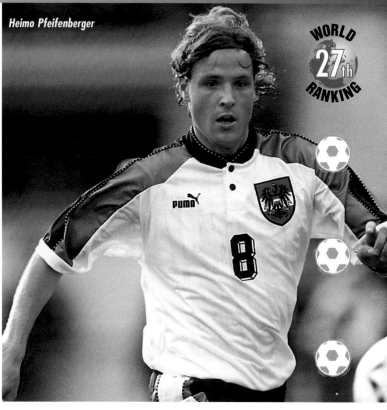
Heimo Pfeifenberger

WORLD 27th RANKING

THE EARLY 1990s WERE NOT A GOOD TIME for Austrian international football. After a poor showing in Italia '90, things went further downhill and they failed to qualify for the European Championships in 1992.

A new coach, former Austrian international midfielder Herbert Prohaska, was appointed in January 1993. But he could not rally the team to another World Cup appearance in the USA in '94, nor to the European Championship in England two years ago.

After this double disappointment Prohaska expected to be dismissed. However, the Osterreichischer Fussball-Bund gave him a vote of confidence and his patient style of management finally paid off with a trip to France. Austria topped Group Four, ahead of

Toni Polster

Scotland – the only side to beat them en route to the finals. Veteran striker Toni Polster was back to his best, scoring a hat-trick in the 3-0 win against Estonia in Tallin – and qualification was ensured with a 4-0 victory over Belarus in Vienna. Other Austrian stars to watch out for are midfield magician Ivica Vastic, defender Heimo Pfeifenberger and playmaker Andi Herzog.

ROUTE TO FRANCE

EUROPEAN QUALIFYING GROUP FOUR
Austria's Results

31.8.96	Austria 0 - Scotland 0
9.10.96	Sweden 0 - Austria 1
9.11.96	Austria 2 - Latvia 1
2.4.97	Scotland 2 - Austria 0
30.4.97	Austria 2 - Estonia 0
8.6.97	Latvia 1 - Austria 3
20.8.97	Estonia 0 - Austria 3
6.9.97	Austria 1 - Sweden 0
10.9.97	Belarus 0 - Austria 1
11.10.97	Austria 4 - Belarus 0

Final Table

	P	W	D	L	F	A	Pts
AUSTRIA	10	8	1	1	17	4	25
Scotland	10	7	2	1	15	3	23
Sweden	10	7	0	3	16	9	21
Latvia	10	3	1	6	10	14	10
Estonia	10	1	1	8	4	16	4
Belarus	10	1	1	8	5	21	4

AUSTRIA FACT FILE

Colours: White shirts, black shorts, black socks
Coach: Herbert Prohaska

WORLD CUP FINALS RECORD

1930	did not enter	1978	2nd round
1934	4th place	1982	2nd round
1938-50	did not enter	1986	did not qualify
1954	3rd place	1990	1st round
1958	1st round	1994	did not qualify
1962-74	did not qualify		

23

FRANCE

GROUP C

FRANCE LAST HIT THE GLORY
trail in 1984, when they won the
European Championship on
home soil with a team
inspired by their great
captain Michel Platini. Back
then Platini, the player,
dominated the tournament
from start to finish. Since
then he has enjoyed a spell
as coach of the national team,
and is now the organising
co-president of this year's
finals. Many French fans see his
involvement as a good omen for
a summer of success.

Indeed, those fans are desperate for
success in the World Cup. The last time
they actually reached the finals stage
was back in 1986 when they finished
third in Mexico. Coached by Aimé
Jacquet since 1993, France got to the
1996 European Championship semi-final
in England and went out in a penalty
shoot-out against the Czech Republic. As
automatic qualifiers this year, they have
obviously not had to endure the rigours
of the qualification competition during
the past fifteen months or so.

Instead France have played a series
of friendly encounters, including a
1-0 defeat by England in Le Tournoi
de France, and a victory over
Scotland last November.
Jacquet's overall record has
been excellent – just two
defeats in 36 matches to
last December.

Yet, for all that, there
seems to be an element of
doubt in the French
sporting press and among
those fervent fans; a doubt
that the national team can
go all the way. That feeling
will surely change with
the approach of the
finals and the
build-up of
excitement and
expectation.

Jacquet
certainly has
some world-
class players
from which

Marcel Desailly

**Automatic
qualification as
World Cup hosts**

to formulate his strongest squad for the serious stuff this summer. Look out for skipper Zinedine Zidane, midfielders Marcel Desailly and Youri Djorkaeff – and the exciting youngster Ibrahim Ba.

Fabien Barthez gives the orders!

Ibrahim Ba

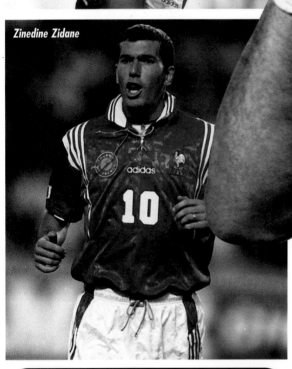

Zinedine Zidane

FRANCE FACT FILE

Colours: Blue shirts, white shorts, red socks
Coach: Aimé Jacquet

WORLD CUP FINALS RECORD			
1930	1st round	1962	did not qualify
1934	1st round	1966	1st round
1938	2nd round	1970-74	did not qualify
1950	did not qualify	1978	1st round
1954	1st round	1982	4th place
1958	3rd place	1986	3rd place
		1990-94	did not qualify

SOUTH AFRICA

WORLD 36th RANKING

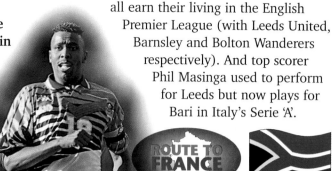

ENGLISH SOCCER FANS GOT A TASTE OF South Africa's footballing prowess when the 'Bafana-Bafana' team came to Old Trafford in May 1997 and gave the home side a torrid time. Although South Africa lost the match 2-1, they left a lasting impression.

Not only was the South African side difficult to beat, but their fans were incredibly enthusiastic and the match was played in a wonderful atmosphere.

Since South Africa's return to political acceptance throughout the world some five years ago, the national soccer squad has gone from strength to strength. Bafana-Bafana's record in around 50 full internationals had seen them shooting into the top 30 in the World Ranking's list (although they later dropped further down the table). And they are the current African Nations Cup holders. Skipper Lucas Radebe, midfielder Eric Tinkler and defender Mark Fish

all earn their living in the English Premier League (with Leeds United, Barnsley and Bolton Wanderers respectively). And top scorer Phil Masinga used to perform for Leeds but now plays for Bari in Italy's Serie 'A'.

ROUTE TO FRANCE

AFRICA GROUP THREE
Final Table

	P	W	D	L	F	A	Pts
SOUTH AFRICA	6	4	1	1	7	3	13
Congo	6	3	1	2	5	5	10
Zambia	6	2	2	2	7	6	8
Rep of Congo	6	0	2	4	4	9	2

SOUTH AFRICA FACT FILE

Colours: Gold, black and white shirts, black shorts, white socks
Coach: Philippe Troussier

WORLD CUP FINALS RECORD
First time qualifiers this year

Lucas Radebe

SAUDI ARABIA

WORLD 32nd RANKING

SAUDI ARABIA BOASTS AN EFFICIENT, youthful and well organised squad – backed by one of the richest nations in the world. In December 1996 they lifted the Asia Cup for a record-equalling third time.

Two years earlier the Saudi side had reached the second round of the World Cup in the

United States, chalking up victories over Belgium and Morocco before crashing out in a 3-1 defeat by Sweden. The central pivot in the Saudi team is skipper and midfield general Khalid Moussad. Also look out for young striker Al Jaber and experienced 'keeper Mohammed Al Dyeyea.

ROUTE TO FRANCE

ASIA SECOND ROUND GROUP A
Final Table

	P	W	D	L	F	A	Pts
SAUDI ARABIA	8	4	2	2	8	6	14
Iran	8	3	3	2	13	8	12
China	8	3	2	3	11	14	11
Qatar	8	3	1	4	7	10	10
Kuwait	8	2	2	4	7	8	8

SAUDI ARABIA FACT FILE

Colours: Green shirts, white shorts, green socks
Coach: Carlos Alberto Parreira

WORLD CUP FINALS RECORD
1930-74	did not enter	1994	2nd round
1978-90	did not qualify		

Al Jaber in action

26

DENMARK

SIX YEARS AGO DENMARK SURPRISED THE entire footballing world by winning the European Championship in Sweden, after 'standing in' for Yugoslavia. They then proceeded to miss out on the World Cup finals of 1994. But now Denmark are back, having made it to France as Group One winners – ahead of Croatia – in a campaign that had its share of ups and downs.

The Danes began well enough, with four wins and a draw, but then lost momentum with a 3-0 defeat in Bosnia. In the end it all came down to the last match. To ensure top spot, Denmark needed a point against Greece in Athens. Super 'keeper Peter Schmeichel turned out to be the hero of the hour, pulling off a brilliant save late in the game to secure a 0-0 scoreline.

Other stars of the Danish squad include the brothers Brian and Michael Laudrup, Per Frandsen of Bolton, Alan Neilsen of Spurs and Celtic's central defender Marc Reiper.

ROUTE TO FRANCE

WORLD 24th RANKING

EUROPEAN QUALIFYING GROUP ONE
Denmark's Results

1.9.96	Slovenia 0 - Denmark 2
9.10.96	Denmark 2 - Greece 1
29.3.97	Croatia 1 - Denmark 1
30.4.97	Denmark 4 - Slovenia 0
8.6.97	Denmark 2 - Bosnia 0
20.8.97	Bosnia 3 - Denmark 0
10.9.97	Denmark 3 - Croatia 1
11.10.97	Greece 0 - Denmark 0

Final Table

	P	W	D	L	F	A	Pts
DENMARK	8	5	2	1	14	6	17
Croatia	8	4	3	1	17	12	15
Greece	8	4	2	2	11	4	14
Bosnia	8	3	0	5	9	14	9
Slovenia	8	0	1	7	5	20	1

DENMARK FACT FILE

Colours: Red shirts, white shorts, red socks
Coach: Bo Johansen

WORLD CUP FINALS RECORD

1930-58	did not qualify	1986	2nd round
1962	did not enter	1990-94	did not qualify
1966-82	did not qualify		

Brian Laudrup

A hair-raising moment for Peter Schmeichel

SPAIN

GROUP D

Amavisca in action against Romania

*Veteran 'keeper
Andoni Zubizaretta*

SPAIN APPEARED IN THE FINALS STAGES of the previous five World Cups, but did not progress beyond the quarter-finals. In 1994, in the USA, they got to the last eight before going out 2-1 to Italy in Boston.

This time around coach Javier Clemente commands one of the strongest squads in the finals. England experienced the might of the Spanish side in the European Championship quarter-finals at Wembley in 1996, when it took a penalty shoot-out to see the home side through to the semis.

Clemente believes that football matches are won by hard work and persistence enlivened by touches of flair. In this, he has toughened up the team. Gone are the days when Spain played pretty football and little else. His squad qualified for this year's World Cup finals with a game to spare in the Group Six campaign.

The stars who will be helping Clemente in his assault on the World Cup should include veteran goalkeeper and captain Andoni

28

SPAIN

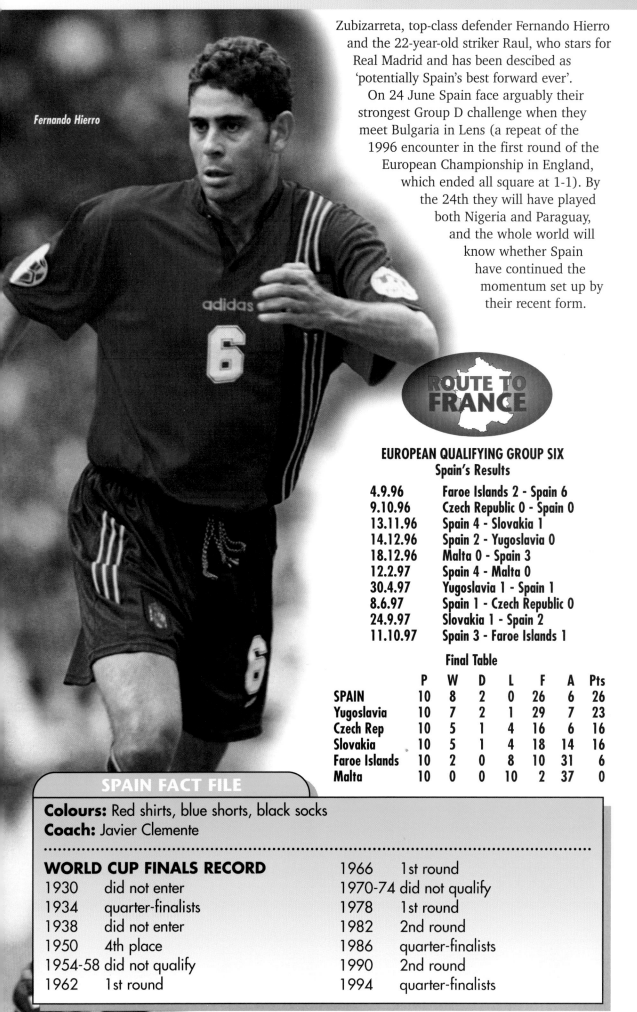

Fernando Hierro

Zubizarreta, top-class defender Fernando Hierro and the 22-year-old striker Raul, who stars for Real Madrid and has been descibed as 'potentially Spain's best forward ever'.

On 24 June Spain face arguably their strongest Group D challenge when they meet Bulgaria in Lens (a repeat of the 1996 encounter in the first round of the European Championship in England, which ended all square at 1-1). By the 24th they will have played both Nigeria and Paraguay, and the whole world will know whether Spain have continued the momentum set up by their recent form.

ROUTE TO FRANCE

EUROPEAN QUALIFYING GROUP SIX
Spain's Results

4.9.96	Faroe Islands 2 - Spain 6
9.10.96	Czech Republic 0 - Spain 0
13.11.96	Spain 4 - Slovakia 1
14.12.96	Spain 2 - Yugoslavia 0
18.12.96	Malta 0 - Spain 3
12.2.97	Spain 4 - Malta 0
30.4.97	Yugoslavia 1 - Spain 1
8.6.97	Spain 1 - Czech Republic 0
24.9.97	Slovakia 1 - Spain 2
11.10.97	Spain 3 - Faroe Islands 1

Final Table

	P	W	D	L	F	A	Pts
SPAIN	10	8	2	0	26	6	26
Yugoslavia	10	7	2	1	29	7	23
Czech Rep	10	5	1	4	16	6	16
Slovakia	10	5	1	4	18	14	16
Faroe Islands	10	2	0	8	10	31	6
Malta	10	0	0	10	2	37	0

SPAIN FACT FILE

Colours: Red shirts, blue shorts, black socks
Coach: Javier Clemente

WORLD CUP FINALS RECORD

1930	did not enter	1966	1st round
1934	quarter-finalists	1970-74	did not qualify
1938	did not enter	1978	1st round
1950	4th place	1982	2nd round
1954-58	did not qualify	1986	quarter-finalists
1962	1st round	1990	2nd round
		1994	quarter-finalists

NIGERIA

67th WORLD RANKING

NIGERIA, ONE OF AFRICA'S STRONGEST footballing nations, are the current Olympic Gold Medallists. Guided by coach Philippe Troussier they qualified for the 1998 World Cup finals with relative ease. Since then, however, Troussier has been succeeded by Bora

ROUTE TO FRANCE

AFRICA GROUP ONE Final Table						
	P	W	D	L	F	A	Pts
NIGERIA	6	4	1	1	10	4	13
Guinea	6	4	0	2	10	5	12
Kenya	6	3	1	2	11	12	10
Burkina Faso	6	0	0	6	7	17	0

NIGERIA FACT FILE

Colours: All green
Coach: Bora Milutinovic
....

WORLD CUP FINALS RECORD

1930-58	did not enter	1994	2nd round
1962-90	did not qualify		

Milutinovic, the man who took Mexico to the finals.

1998 will see Nigeria's second appearance at the World Cup finals. Last time, in the USA, they reached the second round before losing 2-1 to Italy in Boston. This time they could be a real thorn in the side for Spain and Bulgaria. Striker Daniel Amokachi, who won an FA Cup winners' medal with Everton in 1995, was Nigeria's leading scorer during the qualifiers for this year's finals. Another Nigerian star with Premiership experience is Chelsea defender Celestine Babayaro.

Celestine Babayaro (above) and Sunday Oliseh (right)

PARAGUAY

30th WORLD RANKING

PARAGUAY WERE expected to be among the also-rans in the South American Round Robin qualification league. They began with a 1-0 defeat by Colombia – but then surprised everyone with a marvellous unbeaten run of nine matches to keep them within striking distance of the leaders and eventually finish in second place.

Carlos Gamarra

ROUTE TO FRANCE

SOUTH AMERICAN ROUND ROBIN LEAGUE Final Table (Top four qualify)							
	P	W	D	L	F	A	Pts
Argentina	16	8	6	2	23	13	30
PARAGUAY	16	9	2	5	21	14	29
Colombia	16	8	4	4	23	15	28
Chile	16	7	4	5	32	18	25
Peru	16	7	4	5	19	20	25
Ecuador	16	6	3	7	22	21	21
Uruguay	16	6	3	7	18	21	21
Bolivia	16	4	5	7	18	21	17
Venezuela	16	0	3	13	8	41	3

Paraguay's goalkeeper-captain Jose Luis Chilavert should provide some entertaining moments this summer. He is a free-kick expert, and an effective one at that. It was a Chilavert's dead-ball special that earned Paraguay a point in their match against Argentina in Buenos Aires in September 1996. Also look out for sweeper Carlos Gamarra and right wing back Fernando Arce who can deliver a long ball with unerring accuracy.

PARAGUAY FACT FILE

Colours: Red and white striped shirts, blue shorts, blue socks
Coach: Paulo Cesar Carpeggiani
....

WORLD CUP FINALS RECORD

1930	1st round	1958	1st round
1934-38	did not enter	1962-82	did not qualify
1950	1st round	1986	2nd round
1954	did not enter	1990-94	did not qualify

BULGARIA

THE BULGARIAN SQUAD WILL BE AMONG the oldest in this year's finals – that also means one of the most experienced. And they'll be anxious to at least repeat their feat of 1994, when they finished 4th in the USA World Cup.

In progressing from Group D behind Nigeria, the Bulgarians had recorded a famous 2-0 victory over Argentina in Dallas. In the second round they beat Mexico in a penalty shoot-out. In the quarter-finals in New York they recorded their most famous result, a 2-1 win against reigning champions Germany. Elimination came in a 2-1 defeat by Italy in the semi-finals. In the third/fourth place play-off Bulgaria suffered a 4-0 defeat at the hands of Sweden in Los Angeles.

Throughout the finals Bulgaria had proven one of the more durable outfits, and in Hristo Stoichkov they boasted the tournament's joint top scorer with six goals (a tally shared with Russia's Oleg Salenko).

Bulgaria got off to a faltering start in the 1998 World Cup qualifying campaign with a surprise 2-1 defeat in Israel. But six consecutive victories followed to book their passage to France. The sixth of those successes was against

Hristo Stoichkov

Russia, with the winning goal coming from skipper Trifon Ivanov.

Russia beat Bulgaria 4-2 in the last match of the Group Five qualifying programme. But by then it was too late. Bulgaria were uncatchable and the Russians were consigned to the play-offs in which they were eventually beaten by Italy.

ROUTE TO FRANCE

EUROPEAN QUALIFYING GROUP FIVE
Bulgaria's Results

1.9.96	Israel 2 - Bulgaria 1
8.10.96	Luxembourg 1 - Bulgaria 2
14.12.96	Cyprus 1 - Bulgaria 3
2.4.97	Bulgaria 4 - Cyprus 1
8.6.97	Bulgaria 4 - Luxembourg 0
20.8.97	Bulgaria 1 - Israel 0
10.9.97	Bulgaria 1 - Russia 0
11.10.97	Russia 4 - Bulgaria 2

Final Table

	P	W	D	L	F	A	Pts
BULGARIA	8	6	0	2	18	9	18
Russia	8	5	2	1	19	5	17
Israel	8	4	1	3	9	7	13
Cyprus	8	3	1	4	10	15	10
Luxembourg	8	0	0	8	2	22	0

Trifon Ivanov

BULGARIA FACT FILE

Colours: White shirts, green shorts, red socks
Coach: Hristo Bonev

WORLD CUP FINALS RECORD

1930	did not enter	1974	1st round
1934-58	did not qualify	1978-82	did not qualify
1962	1st round	1986	2nd round
1966	1st round	1990	did not qualify
1970	1st round	1994	4th place

WORLD **38th** RANKING

31

WORLD
25th
RANKING

GROUP E

Dennis Bergkamp

Aron Winter

Marc Overmars

32

HOLLAND

HOLLAND ARE GENERALLY REGARDED AS one the best teams never to have won the World Cup. Twice they have been to the final (in 1974 and 1978) and twice they finished second. Coach Guus Hiddink would dearly love to write a new chapter in the history of Dutch soccer by lifting the World Cup this summer.

He certainly has some superb talent to work with. The Arsenal pair Dennis Bergkamp and Marc Overmars are players of true quality. So too are Patrick Kluivert, Clarence Seedorf, Edgar Davids, Aron Winter and the De Boer twins Ronald and Frank. All of these Dutch

stars would dearly love to experience real success on the world stage.

Two emphatic victories over Wales (3-1 and 7-1) got Holland off to a great start in the qualifying campaign for the 1998 finals. This was followed by a 3-0 win against neighbours Belgium and a 4-0 drubbing of little San Marino.

Everything seemed to be going to plan for the orange-shirted team. Then a missed penalty in Turkey contributed to three dropped points and an anxious time in the Dutch camp. But things got back on track with a 6-0 drubbing of San Marino and a second victory over Belgium. Eventually Holland qualified as Group Seven winners, one point ahead of Belgium.

Holland are now matched again with neighbours Belgium in Group E, in the Stade de France on 13 June. That game, between the two nations who will jointly host the next European Championship in the year 2000, will be as keenly contested as a local derby.

Edgar Davids

ROUTE TO FRANCE

EUROPEAN QUALIFYING GROUP SEVEN
Holland's Results

5.10.96	Wales 1 - Holland 3
9.11.96	Holland 7 - Wales 1
14.12.96	Belgium 0 - Holland 3
29.3.97	Holland 4 - San Marino 0
2.4.97	Turkey 1 - Holland 0
30.4.97	San Marino 0 - Holland 6
6.9.97	Holland 3 - Belgium 1
11.10.97	Holland 0 - Turkey 0

Final Table

	P	W	D	L	F	A	Pts
HOLLAND	8	6	1	1	26	4	19
Belgium	8	6	0	2	20	11	18
Turkey	8	4	2	2	21	9	14
Wales	8	2	1	5	20	21	7
San Marino	8	0	0	8	0	42	0

HOLLAND FACT FILE

Colours: Orange shirts, white shorts, orange socks
Coach: Guus Hiddink

WORLD CUP FINALS RECORD
1930	did not enter
1934	1st round
1938	1st round
1950-54	did not enter
1958-70	did not qualify
1974	RUNNERS-UP
1978	RUNNERS-UP
1982-86	did not qualify
1990	2nd round
1994	quarter-finalists

33

BELGIUM

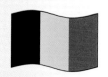

WORLD **41**st RANKING

Enzo Scifo

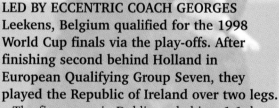

Luc Nilis

LED BY ECCENTRIC COACH GEORGES Leekens, Belgium qualified for the 1998 World Cup finals via the play-offs. After finishing second behind Holland in European Qualifying Group Seven, they played the Republic of Ireland over two legs.

The first game in Dublin ended in a 1-1 draw, giving the initiative to Belgium. In the 25th minute of the return leg in Brussels, Luis Oliveira opened the scoring for Belgium. Ray Houghton replied in the 58th and the Irish were right back in the game.

The match turned on a throw-in, in line with the Irish penalty area. The Irish players were convinced that a Belgian had put the ball out, but the throw was awarded to Belgium. Boffin threw to Verheyen who nodded the ball on to Classens who flicked it on to Luc Nilis who stroked it into the Irish net. With that one swift, efficient move following a highly debated decision, Mick McCarthy's side were knocked out of the competition. Belgium will be making their fifth successive appearance in the finals stages of the World Cup. Leekens and his men would love to better their 1986 performance, when Belgium finished fourth in Mexico.

EUROPEAN QUALIFYING GROUP SEVEN
Belgium's Results

31.8.96	Belgium 2 - Turkey 1
9.10.96	San Marino 0 - Belgium 3
14.12.96	Belgium 0 - Holland 3
29.3.97	Wales 1 - Belgium 2
30.4.97	Turkey 1 - Belgium 3
7.6.97	Belgium 6 - San Marino 0
6.9.97	Holland 3 - Belgium 1
11.10.97	Belgium 3 - Wales 2

Final Table

	P	W	D	L	F	A	Pts
Holland	8	6	1	1	26	4	19
Belgium	8	6	0	2	20	11	18
Turkey	8	4	2	2	21	9	14
Wales	8	2	1	5	20	21	7
San Marino	8	0	0	8	0	42	0

PLAY-OFFS

29.10.97	Republic of Ireland 1 - Belgium 1
15.11.97	Belgium 2 - Republic of Ireland 1

BELGIUM FACT FILE

Colours: All red
Coach: Georges Leekens

WORLD CUP FINALS RECORD

1930	1st round	1970	1st round
1934	1st round	1974-78	did not qualify
1938	1st round	1982	2nd round
1950	did not enter	1986	4th place
1954	1st round	1990	2nd round
1958-66	did not qualify	1994	1st round

SOUTH KOREA ARE MAKING their fourth successive World Cup finals appearance. They qualified with three games left to play and finished six points ahead of closest rivals Japan. If they continue in the kind of form that took them to the finals, South Korea could well progress beyond the opening round for the first time.

South Korea traditionally give the Number 10 shirt to their most inspirational player, an honour currently held by prolific goalscorer Choi Young-su. Also look out for teenage midfield star Ko Jong-so and defender Hong Myung-bo, who represented his country in the Rest of the World squad at the World Cup draw in Marseille last December.

Whatever the outcome of South Korea's adventures in 1998 they will most definitely be part of the next World Cup finals, as they will jointly host the 2002 event with Japan. It will the first time ever that the tournament has been staged on a shared basis, and the first time the World Cup finals have been staged in Asia – a fact which underlines the fast-growing stature of soccer in the Far East.

Hong Myung-Bo

ASIA SECOND ROUND GROUP B
Final Table

	P	W	D	L	F	A	Pts
SOUTH KOREA	8	6	1	1	19	7	19
Japan	8	3	4	3	17	9	13
UAE	8	2	3	3	9	12	9
Uzbekistan	8	1	3	4	13	18	6
Kazakhstan	8	1	3	4	7	19	6

SOUTH KOREA FACT FILE

Colours: All red
Coach: Cha Bum Kun

WORLD CUP FINALS RECORD

1930-50	did not enter	1986	1st round
1954	1st round	1990	1st round
1958-82	did not qualify	1994	1st round

MEXICO QUALIFIED FOR the 1998 World Cup finals, despite only managing a draw in each of their last three games in the CONCACAF programme. After the 0-0 result against ten-men USA in the Azteca Stadium in November 1997, the Mexican side was booed off the pitch.

In the next game against Costa Rica, also in the Azteca, Mexico allowed a 3-1 lead to slide into a 3-3 draw. The programme was completed with a 0-0 draw in Jamaica. Mexico had qualified, but the string of disappointing results in the latter stages led to the sacking of coach Bora Milutinovic. A new coach, Manuel Lapuente, was appointed to guide Mexico through their eleventh World Cup finals campaign – and to aim higher than the second round finish of 1994.

Mexico's 'keeper George Campos!

CONCACAF FINAL QUALIFYING LEAGUE
Final Table (Top three qualify)

	P	W	D	L	F	A	Pts
MEXICO	10	4	6	0	23	7	18
USA	10	4	5	1	17	9	17
Jamaica	10	3	5	2	7	12	14
Costa Rica	10	3	3	4	13	12	12
El Salvador	10	2	4	4	11	16	10
Canada	10	1	3	6	5	20	6

MEXICO FACT FILE

Colours: Green shirts, white shorts, red socks
Coach: Manuel Lapuente

WORLD CUP FINALS RECORD

1930	1st round	1970	quarter-finalists
1934	did not qualify	1974	did not qualify
1938	did not enter	1978	1st round
1950	1st round	1982	did not qualify
1954	1st round	1986	quarter-finalists
1958	1st round	1990	did not enter
1962	1st round	1994	2nd round
1966	1st round		

GERMANY

Jürgen Klinsmann – the skipper smiles

WORLD 2nd RANKING

TWO YEARS AGO GERMANY WON THE European Championship, beating the Czech Republic in the final at Wembley with the only 'Golden Goal' of the entire tournament. It was the third time Germany had been crowned Champions of Europe.

Now they are aiming to add to their trophy collection by winning the World Cup for a fourth time. The last time they were World Champions was in the Italia '90 final against Argentina.

Everyone knows that the Germans traditionally put out one of Europe's strongest teams, a fact underlined by their standing at second place in the world rankings. Yet, like

Andreas Kopke

GROUP F

GERMANY FACT FILE

Colours: White shirts, black shorts, white socks
Coach: Berti Vogts

WORLD CUP FINALS RECORD

Year	Result	Year	Result
1930	did not enter	1970	3rd place
1934	3rd place	1974	**WORLD CHAMPIONS**
1938	1st round	1978	2nd round
1950	did not enter	1982	**RUNNERS-UP**
1954	**WORLD CHAMPIONS**	1986	**RUNNERS-UP**
1958	4th place	1990	**WORLD CHAMPIONS**
1962	quarter-finalists	1994	quarter-finalists
1966	**RUNNERS-UP**		• *1950-90 record for West Germany*

36

Italy, they made rather heavy weather of qualifying for this year's finals, particularly in the last crucial match against Albania. Germany eventually won 4-3 to ensure a table-topping finish, but it had been a close run thing with Ukraine and Portugal.

Coach Berti Vogts will now turn his attention towards Group F opponents Yugoslavia, Iran and the United States – none of them particularly easy opponents. But his team will employ its usual dogged determination, strength and skill and are almost bound to progress beyond the Group stage. After that few will be surprised if Germany reach the final again this year.

The German squad includes some of Europe's top talent. In the striking department are prolific scorer Olivier Bierhoff and skipper Jürgen Klinsmann. Then there is newcomer Olaf Marschall who plays for Kaiserslauten and is one of the Bundesliga's top scorers. Thomas Hassler commands things from right midfield. Andreas Kopke is one of the world's top 'keepers. And, in defence, look out for Kohler and Linke. The sweeper role is usually occupied by Matthias Sammer, but he has been injured and looks unlikely to make the finals, which will be a great loss for Germany.

ROUTE TO FRANCE

EUROPEAN QUALIFYING GROUP NINE
Germany's Results

9.10.96	Armenia 1 - Germany 5
9.11.96	Germany 1 - N. Ireland 1
14.12.96	Portugal 0 - Germany 0
2.4.97	Albania 2 - Germany 3
30.4.97	Germany 2 - Ukraine 0
7.6.97	Ukraine 0 - Germany 0
20.8.97	N. Ireland 1 - Germany 3
6.9.97	Germany 1 - Portugal 1
10.9.97	Germany 4 - Armenia 0
11.10.97	Germany 4 - Albania 3

Final Table

	P	W	D	L	F	A	Pts
GERMANY	10	6	4	0	23	9	22
Ukraine	10	6	2	2	10	6	20
Portugal	10	5	4	1	12	4	19
Armenia	10	1	5	4	8	17	8
N. Ireland	10	1	4	5	6	10	7
Albania	10	1	1	8	7	20	4

Thomas Hassler

USA

WORLD 12th RANKING

SINCE STAGING THE LAST World Cup finals in 1994 – and reaching the second round into the bargain, the USA has earned great respect as a footballing power. This fact was underlined by the magnificent 0-0 draw against Mexico, in the frenzied atmosphere of the packed Azteca Stadium in November 1997. The American team held on against all the odds and despite having Jeff Agoos sent-off in the first half.

The result revitalised the USA's qualification campaign. A 3-0 defeat of Canada and a 4-2 victory over El Salvador sealed second place in the CONCACAF table. In February the USA's confidence was boosted by a magnificent 1-0 home win over

John Harkes

world champions Brazil. The USA open in Group F against Germany at the Parc des Princes in Paris on 15 June.

CONCACAF FINAL QUALIFYING LEAGUE
Final Table (Top three qualify)

	P	W	D	L	F	A	Pts
Mexico	10	4	6	0	23	7	18
USA	10	4	5	1	17	9	17
Jamaica	10	3	5	2	7	12	14
Costa Rica	10	3	3	4	13	12	12
El Salvador	10	2	4	4	11	16	10
Canada	10	1	3	6	5	20	6

USA FACT FILE

Colours: White shirts, blue shorts, white socks
Coach: Steve Sampson

WORLD CUP FINALS RECORD

1930	semi-finalists	1954-86	did not qualify
1934	1st round	1990	1st round
1938	did not enter	1994	2nd round
1950	1st round		

IRAN

WORLD 47th RANKING

38

Khodadad Azizi

THE VERY LAST goal of the entire qualifying tournament secured Iran's place in France this summer. It was scored by the Asian Footballer of the Year, Khodadad Azizi, in the 80th

minute of the second-leg of the Asia/Oceania play-off against Australia. In the first-leg, in Tehran, the 'Socceroos' had held Iran to a 1-1 draw and were favourites to go through.

In the return match, played in front of an 85,000 crowd at the Melbourne Cricket Ground, Terry Venables' side appeared to be coasting to qualification, having gone 2-0 up within 35 minutes. It was a remarkable comeback that took Iran to their second World Cup finals. With just 14 minutes left, Karim Bagheri pounced on a mistake in the Aussie defence to reduce the arrears. And when Azizi produced his little piece of magic for a 2-2 draw, Iran qualified on the away goals ruling.

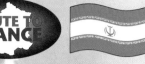

ASIA SECOND ROUND GROUP A
Final Table

	P	W	D	L	F	A	Pts
Saudi Arabia	8	4	2	2	8	6	14
IRAN	8	3	3	2	13	8	12
China	8	3	2	3	11	14	11
Qatar	8	3	1	4	7	10	10
Kuwait	8	2	2	4	7	8	8

PLAY-OFF
(in Malaysia)
16.11.97   Japan 3 - Iran 2
ASIA/OCEANIA PLAY-OFF
22.11.97   Iran 1 - Australia 1
29.11.97   Australia 2 - Iran 2
(Iran won on away goals rule)

IRAN FACT FILE

Colours: Green shirts, white shorts, red socks
Coach: Tomislav Ivic

WORLD CUP FINALS RECORD

1930-70	did not enter	1982-86	did not enter
1974	did not qualify	1990-94	did not qualify
1978	1st round		

YUGOSLAVIA

IN THE EARLY 1990s THE POLITICAL situation in the Balkans saw Yugoslavia's isolation from FIFA – and caused their withdrawal from the 1992 European Championship.

Yugoslavia has since returned to the FIFA fold

and are once again proving themselves one of the classiest of Europe's leading football-playing nations. Under coach Slobodan Santrac they qualified for the finals via the play-offs, after finishing behind Spain in Group Six.

Play-off opponents, Hungary, didn't know what hit them in the first leg in Budapest. The Yugoslavs were rampant as they chalked up an astonishing 7-1 victory. The job was completed in the second leg with a 5-0 victory and a 12-1 aggregate.

The Yugoslavian squad is built around a solid defence, a midfield masterminded by Dragan Stojkovic and an exciting attack led by Dejan Savicevic, Savo Milosevic and Pedrag Mijatovic.

Dragan Stojkovic

Pedrag Mijatovic

EUROPEAN QUALIFYING GROUP SIX
Yugoslavia's Results

24.4.96	Yugoslavia 3 - Faroe Islands 1
2.6.96	Yugoslavia 6 - Malta 0
6.10.96	Faroe Islands 1 - Yugoslavia 8
10.11.96	Yugoslavia 1 - Czech Republic 0
14.12.96	Spain 2 - Yugoslavia 0
2.4.97	Czech Republic 1 - Yugoslavia 2
30.4.97	Yugoslavia 1 - Spain 1
8.6.97	Yugoslavia 2 - Slovakia 0
10.9.97	Slovakia 1 - Yugoslavia 1
11.10.97	Malta 0 - Yugoslavia 5

Final Table

	P	W	D	L	F	A	Pts
Spain	10	8	2	0	26	6	26
YUGOSLAVIA	10	7	2	1	29	7	23
Czech Rep	10	5	1	4	16	6	16
Slovakia	10	5	1	4	18	14	16
Faroe Islands	10	2	0	8	10	31	6
Malta	10	0	0	10	2	37	0

PLAY-OFFS

29.10.97	Hungary 1 - Yugoslavia 7
15.11.97	Yugoslavia 5 - Hungary 0

YUGOSLAVIA FACT FILE

Colours: Blue shirts, white shorts, red socks
Coach: Slobodan Santrac

WORLD CUP FINALS RECORD

Year	Result	Year	Result
1930	semi-finalists	1974	2nd round
1934-38	did not qualify	1978	did not qualify
1950	1st round	1982	1st round
1954	quarter-finalists	1986	did not qualify
1958	quarter-finalists	1990	quarter-finalists
1962	4th place	1994	did not enter
1966-70	did not qualify		

ROMANIA

OF ALL THE EUROPEAN QUALIFIERS FOR the 1998 World Cup finals, Romania finished with the best record, topping Group Eight unbeaten and with a marvellous goals difference tally of +33. They were the first European side to book a ticket to the finals. And it was only in the last match of the campaign – a 1-1 draw with the Republic of Ireland – that they dropped any points at all.

This highly successful qualifying campaign makes Romania one of the favourites to go all the way this summer. They begin by facing up to the flamboyant Colombian side in Lyon on 15 June; Romania then take on England, arguably the strongest of the 'second string' nations, in Toulouse on the 22nd. This promises to be one of *the* matches of the tournament and is eagerly awaited by fans and players of both teams.

Romania's star players include Marius Lacatus and Gica Popescu, Chelsea wing-back Dan Petrescu and midfield maestros Dorinel Muntaneau and Gheorghe Hagi, a player who has been compared at his best to the great Argentinian star Diego Maradona.

Gheorghe Hagi

GROUP G

ROUTE TO FRANCE

EUROPEAN QUALIFYING GROUP EIGHT
Romania's Results

31.8.96	Romania 3 - Lithuania 0
9.10.96	Iceland 0 - Romania 4
14.12.96	Macedonia 0 - Romania 3
29.3.97	Romania 8 - Liechtenstein 0
2.4.97	Lithuania 0 - Romania 1
30.4.97	Romania 1 - Rep of Ireland 0
20.8.97	Romania 4 - Macedonia 2
6.9.97	Liechtenstein 1 - Romania 8
10.9.97	Romania 4 - Iceland 0
11.10.97	Rep of Ireland 1 - Romania 1

Final Table

	P	W	D	L	F	A	Pts
ROMANIA	10	9	1	0	37	4	28
Rep of Ireland	10	5	3	2	22	8	18
Lithuania	10	5	2	3	11	8	17
Macedonia	10	4	1	5	22	18	13
Iceland	10	2	3	5	11	16	9
Liechtenstein	10	0	0	10	3	52	0

ROMANIA FACT FILE

Colours: Yellow shirts, blue shorts, red socks
Coach: Victor Piturca

WORLD CUP FINALS RECORD

1930	1st round
1934	1st round
1938	1st round
1950	did not enter
1954-58	did not qualify
1962	did not enter
1966	did not qualify
1970	1st round
1974-86	did not qualify
1990	2nd round
1994	quarter-finalists

ROMANIA

TOTALLY 100%
WORLD
CUP 98
UNOFFICIAL

Dan Petrescu

Gica Popescu

ENGLAND

MANY FOOTBALL EXPERTS BELIEVE THAT England now have their best chance in years to win the World Cup and rekindle the glory days of 1966. Certainly, if they show the kind of resiliance and spirit displayed in their final qualifying game for this year's finals, then Glenn Hoddle's men will be very hard to beat.

David Beckham

That stirring match is now etched on the memory of every red-blooded England fan. In order to ensure qualification and avoid the nail-biting tension of the play-offs England needed at least a draw against Italy in Rome on 11 October 1997. To take on one of the best footballing nations in the world, on their own territory, and come away with the desired result was a daunting task.

A 1-0 defeat by Italy eight months earlier had been the only 'blip' so far in Glenn Hoddle's masterplan. The campaign began back in September 1996, in Moldova. This was Hoddle's first game in charge of the national squad and Alan Shearer's first appearance as England's captain, and it proved a triumph for both men. Nick Barmby opened England's account in the 23rd minute when he belted a Gary Neville cross into the top

England's skipper Alan Shearer

ENGLAND

*England's playmaker,
Paul Gascoigne*

corner of the Moldovan net. Two minutes later Paul Gascoigne made it 2-0 with a well-taken header. Skipper Shearer put the result beyond doubt with a lobbed goal in the 61st minute.

Within six minutes of the kick-off of England's first home game of the campaign, Marek Citko shocked a packed Wembley by putting Poland ahead after some sloppy English defending. Alan Shearer was England's saviour with two trademark goals, in the 24th and 37th minutes. The second was a super strike from 20 yards and was later described by Glenn Hoddle as being 'straight out of the Bobby Charlton Scrapbook'.

Next, England were off to Tbilisi in Georgia. Shearer was out through injury, but the two-pronged strike-force of Teddy Sheringham and Les Ferdinand did the job in his absence: both scored in the 2-0 victory.

Then came that slip-up against Italy on 12 February. The 1-0 defeat went into the record books as England's first ever defeat in a World Cup tie at Wembley. From now on only a 100 per cent effort would be good enough if England were to make it to France as Group winners.

England's challenge got back on course at Wembley on 30 April, with a hard won 2-0 victory over Georgia, in a performance descibed by Glenn Hoddle as 'a bit iffy at times'. The opening goal came from a Teddy Sheringham header just before half time. The second came in injury time from a well-worked indirect free-kick inside the Georgian penalty area. Sheringham back-heeled the ball to Shearer who blasted it into the top of the net.

For their sixth match of the qualifying campaign, England went to Poland where they had not won in 31 years. That tradition was well and truly broken with a 2-0 victory – the goals

43

TOTALLY 100%
WORLD CUP 98
UNOFFICIAL

*Paul Ince was the superhero in a team of heroes
in England's vital 0-0 draw in Italy*

coming from Shearer and Sheringham.

England's World Cup challenge was brilliantly boosted at Wembley on 10 September, with a convincing 4-0 win over Moldova. Paul Scholes headed the opening goal in the 28th minute. Ian Wright scored twice, and Paul Gasgoigne got his name on the scoresheet with a magnificent solo goal. Man-of-the-match Gazza later acknowledged his performance as one of his best ever for England.

Meanwhile, Italy had drawn their penultimate qualifier in Georgia – and England moved to the top of the Group Two table. The stage was set for the Big Showdown in Rome's Olympic Stadium on 11 October.

In the build-up to the game, there was much talk of injuries and other worries in the England camp and a cloak of secrecy was draped over Hoddle's selection. After all the rumours and speculation, the line-up against the 'Azzurri' was a strong one, well-equipped to complete the task

Paul Scholes

Sol Campbell

in hand. The team was: Seaman; Campbell, Le Saux, Ince, Adams, Southgate, Beckham, Gascoigne, Wright, Sheringham and Batty. Nicky Butt came on for Gazza in the 88th minute.

Skippered by Liverpool ace Paul Ince, the lionheart army battled for every ball and never allowed the Italians to settle to their usual fluid game. Ince encouraged, cajoled, inspired and performed miracles in midfield. Caught by Albertini's wayward elbow early in the first half, he left the field for seven minutes and came back with his head swathed in a bandage – there was no way that Paul Ince would allow himself to be substituted in this vital encounter.

Apart from a couple of shaky moments England hardly put a foot wrong. It was a masterful team performance that secured the necessary point with a 0-0 scoreline.

The Three Lions badge will now grace a World Cup finals for the first time since 1990. But Glenn Hoddle and his squad aren't celebrating yet. The champagne is still on ice. The job is only half done.

A decisive result in the opening game against Tunisia in Marseille on 15 June is vital, as Romania in Toulouse on the 22nd and Colombia in Lens on the 26th are both tougher prospects. But if England can continue the good work so far achieved under Glenn Hoddle's leadership, then the experts' predictions might well prove correct.

*David Seaman
– one of the
world's best
'keepers*

ENGLAND FACT FILE

Colours: White shirts, navy shorts, white socks
Coach: Glenn Hoddle

WORLD CUP FINALS RECORD			
1930-38	did not enter	1970	quarter-finalists
1950	1st round	1974-78	did not qualify
1954	quarter-finalists	1982	2nd round
1958	1st round	1986	quarter-finalists
1962	quarter-finalists	1990	4th place
1966	**WORLD CHAMPIONS**	1994	did not qualify

TOTALLY 100%
WORLD CUP 98
UNOFFICIAL

Graeme Le Saux

ROUTE TO FRANCE

EUROPEAN QUALIFYING GROUP TWO
England's Results

1.9.96	Moldova 0 - England 3
9.10.96	England 2 - Poland 1
9.11.96	Georgia 0 - England 2
12.2.97	England 0 - Italy 1
30.4.97	England 2 - Georgia 0
31.5.97	Poland 0 - England 2
10.9.97	England 4 - Moldova 0
11.10.97	Italy 0 - England 0

Final Table

	P	W	D	L	F	A	Pts
ENGLAND	8	6	1	1	15	2	19
Italy	8	5	3	0	11	1	18
Poland	8	3	1	4	10	12	10
Georgia	8	3	1	4	7	9	10
Moldova	8	0	0	8	2	21	0

Complete this chart when England's squad is announced

1. _____
2. _____
3. _____
4. _____
5. _____
6. _____
7. _____
8. _____
9. _____
10. _____
11. _____
12. _____
13. _____
14. _____
15. _____
16. _____
17. _____
18. _____
19. _____
20. _____
21. _____
22. _____

47

COLOMBIA

COLOMBIA, WHO QUALIFIED FOR the 1998 World Cup finals by finishing third in the South American Round Robin League, are England's most unpredictable opponents in Group G.

At their best they have been compared to Brazil. At their worst they can be erratic and ill-tempered performers. But one thing is for sure, Colombia are always skilful and entertaining (who can forget Rene Higuita's 'scorpion kick' against England at Wembley in 1995?).

The squad, coached by Hernan Dario Gomez, boasts such star names as midfielder Carlos Valderrama who has now played in more than 100 internationals, Freddy Rincon, Anthony De Avila and the flamboyant and unpredictable Faustino Asprilla.

Freddy Rincon

Carlos Valderrama

ROUTE TO FRANCE

SOUTH AMERICAN ROUND ROBIN LEAGUE
Final Table (Top four qualify)

	P	W	D	L	F	A	Pts
Argentina	16	8	6	2	23	13	30
Paraguay	16	9	2	5	21	14	29
COLOMBIA	16	8	4	4	23	15	28
Chile	16	7	4	5	32	18	25
Peru	16	7	4	5	19	20	25
Ecuador	16	6	3	7	22	21	21
Uruguay	16	6	3	7	18	21	21
Bolivia	16	4	5	7	18	21	17
Venezuela	16	0	3	13	8	41	3

COLUMBIA FACT FILE

Colours: Yellow shirts, blue shorts, yellow socks
Coach: Hernan Dario Gomez

WORLD CUP FINALS RECORD

1930-54	did not enter	1966-86	did not qualify
1958	did not qualify	1990	2nd round
1962	1st round	1994	1st round

TUNISIA

WORLD 19th RANKING

AFRICA GROUP TWO
Final Table

	P	W	D	L	F	A	Pts
TUNISIA	6	5	1	0	10	1	16
Egypt	6	3	1	2	15	5	10
Liberia	6	1	1	4	2	10	4
Namibia	6	1	1	4	6	17	4

Adel Sellimi

Skander Souayeh

ENGLAND AND TUNISIA HAVE MET JUST once in the past, producing a 1-1 draw in Tunis in 1990. But their current coach, Henryk Kasperczak, will look back on another encounter and perhaps regard it as a good omen for the Class of '98.

Way back in 1973 Kasperczak was a member of the hard-working Polish team that eliminated England from the World Cup qualifiers. He would love to write a similar chapter in France this summer.

Tunisia arrive in France with an impressive unbeaten record in the qualifying stages. Among their victims were Egypt, beaten 1-0 in Tunis and held to an all-important draw in Cairo. They rounded up the campaign with a 4-0 demolition of Namibia and finished six points ahead of Egypt.

Henryk Kasperczak and his squad are now looking forward to meeting England in Marseille on 15 June.

TUNISIA FACT FILE

Colours: Red shirts, white shorts, red socks
Coach: Henryk Kasperczak

WORLD CUP FINALS RECORD

1930-58	did not enter	1978	1st round
1962-74	did not qualify	1982-94	did not qualify

49

ARGENTINA

WORLD 17th RANKING

GROUP H

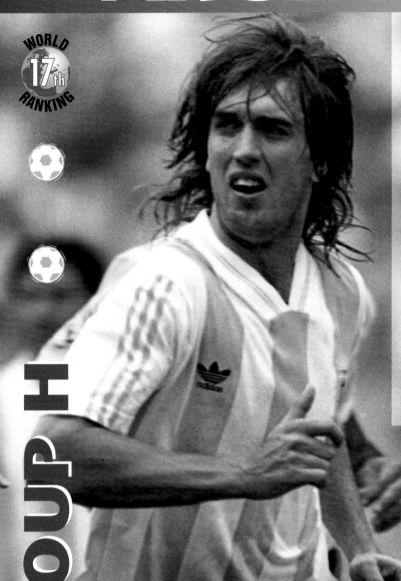

ARGENTINA HAVE TWICE WON THE World Cup and have twice been runners-up in the competition. In 1994 they were eliminated in the second round by Romania – and are now anxious to restore their reputation as one of the world's top soccer-playing nations.

After a decidely shaky start, and amid internal squabbles, Daniel Passarella's side got its act together and eventually qualified for the 1998 World Cup finals as winners of the South American Round Robin table.

The squad includes Argentina's record scorer Gabriel Batistuta, one of the world's top strikers, who plays for Fiorentina in Italy. Among other squad members who earn their living in Italy's Serie 'A' are Hernan Crespo of Parma, and Juan Sebastian Veron of Sampdoria. Ariel Ortega plays for Valencia in Spain and Fernando Redondo plays for Real Madrid.

Now Croatia pose the biggest threat to Argentina's progress. By the time they meet in Bordeaux on 26 June, both teams will have

Superstriker, Gabriel Batistuta

ARGENTINA FACT FILE

Colours: Pale blue and white striped shirts, black shorts, white socks
Coach: Daniel Passarella

WORLD CUP FINALS RECORD			
1930	**RUNNERS-UP**	1970	did not qualify
1934	1st round	1974	2nd round
1938-54	did not qualify	1978	**WORLD CHAMPIONS**
1958	1st round	1982	2nd round
1962	1st round	1986	**WORLD CHAMPIONS**
1966	quarter-finalists	1990	**RUNNERS-UP**
		1994	2nd round

Hernan Crespo

Fernando Redondo

played Jamaica and Japan. And if things go according to expectation in Groups G and H, then the Argentina v Croatia fixture should be a doubly fascinating encounter – especially for England fans. Glenn Hoddle's men could meet either of those teams in the Second Round, in Bordeaux or Saint-Etienne.

ROUTE TO FRANCE

SOUTH AMERICA ROUND ROBIN LEAGUE
Argentina's Results

24.4.96	Argentina 3 - Bolivia 1
2.6.96	Ecuador 2 - Argentina 0
7.7.96	Peru 0 - Argentina 0
1.9.96	Argentina 1 - Paraguay 1
9.10.96	Venezuela 2 - Argentina 5
15.12.96	Argentina 1 - Chile 1
12.1.97	Uruguay 0 - Argentina 0
12.2.97	Colombia 0 - Argentina 1
2.4.97	Bolivia 2 - Argentina 1
30.4.97	Argentina 2 - Ecuador 1
8.6.97	Argentina 2 - Peru 0
6.7.97	Paraguay 1 - Argentina 2
20.7.97	Argentina 2 - Venezuela 0
10.9.97	Chile 1 - Argentina 2
12.10.97	Argentina 0 - Uruguay 0
16.11.97	Argentina 1 - Colombia 1

Final Table (Top four qualify)

	P	W	D	L	F	A	Pts
ARGENTINA	16	8	6	2	23	13	30
Paraguay	16	9	2	5	21	14	29
Colombia	16	8	4	4	23	15	28
Chile	16	7	4	5	32	18	25
Peru	16	7	4	5	19	20	25
Ecuador	16	6	3	7	22	21	21
Uruguay	16	6	3	7	18	21	21
Bolivia	16	4	5	7	18	21	17
Venezuela	16	0	3	13	8	41	3

JAPAN

WORLD 9th RANKING

A 'GOLDEN GOAL' TOOK JAPAN TO France. It came late in extra time in the Asian Zone play-off against Iran, in Jahor Bahru, Malaysia. After 90 minutes the scoreline stood at 2-2, meaning the result would be settled by the sudden death ruling; i.e. the next team to score would win the game.

Twenty-eight minutes of agonising extra time passed before substitute Masayuki Okano became a national hero, when he latched onto a rebound to score the goal that took Japan to the World Cup finals for the first time in 44 years of trying. Okano is a hero, but it is coach Takeshi Okada who is credited with steering Japan to France. He was given the job midway through the qualifying campaign and his shrewd use of tactics

turned the team into winners. Whatever happens to the Japanese in France, they are assured of a place at the 2002 finals – they will jointly host that tournament with South Korea.

ROUTE TO FRANCE

ASIA SECOND ROUND GROUP B
Final Table

	P	W	D	L	F	A	Pts
South Korea	8	6	1	1	19	7	19
JAPAN	8	3	4	1	17	9	13
UAE	8	2	3	3	9	12	9
Uzbekistan	8	1	3	4	13	18	6
Kazakhstan	8	1	3	4	7	19	6

PLAY-OFF
(in Malaysia)
16.11.97   Japan 3 - Iran 2
(Japan won on Golden Goal rule)

JAPAN FACT FILE

Colours: Blue shirts, white shorts, blue socks
Coach: Takeshi Okada

WORLD CUP FINALS RECORD
First time qualifiers this year

Hisashi Kurosaki

JAMAICA

WORLD 33rd RANKING

52

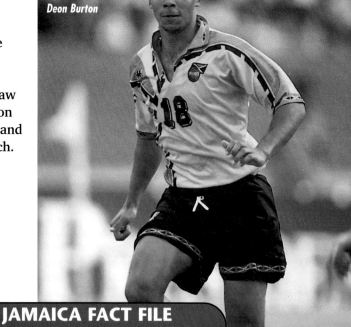
Deon Burton

JAMAICA HAVE MADE IT TO FRANCE AS the first English-speaking Caribbean nation ever to qualify for the World Cup finals. The 'Reggae Boyz' achieved the 'impossible' by finishing third in the CONCACAF qualifying table, behind Mexico and the USA. A 0-0 draw with Mexico in Kingston secured qualification and sparked some remarkable celebrations and a national holiday on the day after the match.

The architect of Jamaica's remarkable success is coach Rene Simoes, a Brazilian who has instilled some steel and discipline in the squad, which includes Wimbledon's Robbie Earle and Derby County striker (and Ronaldo lookalike) Deon Burton.

ROUTE TO FRANCE

CONCACAF FINAL QUALIFYING LEAGUE
Final Table (Top three qualify)

	P	W	D	L	F	A	Pts
Mexico	10	4	6	0	23	7	18
USA	10	4	5	1	17	9	17
JAMAICA	10	3	5	2	7	12	14
Costa Rica	10	3	3	4	13	12	12
El Salvador	10	2	4	4	11	16	10
Canada	10	1	3	6	5	20	6

JAMAICA FACT FILE

Colours: Green shirts, black shorts, green socks
Coach: Rene Simoes

WORLD CUP FINALS RECORD
First time qualifiers this year

CROATIA

WORLD **16th** RANKING

Slaven Bilic

TWO YEARS AGO CROATIA WERE ONE OF the most impressive teams in the European Championship finals in England. They reached the quarter-finals before elimination by Germany. In that match striker Davor Suker scored one of the best goals of the entire tournament.

The Croatian squad has since maintained that consistency to qualify for the current World Cup finals. But they did it the hard way – via the play-offs after finishing runners-up to Denmark in European Qualifying Group One. In the play-offs, they beat Ukraine with an impressive 2-0 victory at home and a 1-1 draw away. Before these two matches coach Miroslav Blazevic consulted an astrologer who assured him that Croatia's World Cup progress was in the stars! Besides Davor Suker, look out for Zvonimir Boban, Alen Boksic, Slaven Bilic and Aljosa Asanovic.

Alen Boksic

ROUTE TO FRANCE

EUROPEAN QUALIFYING GROUP ONE
Croatia's Results

8.10.96	Bosnia 1 - Croatia 4
10.11.96	Croatia 1 - Greece 1
29.3.97	Croatia 1 - Denmark 1
2.4.97	Croatia 3 - Slovenia 3
30.4.97	Greece 0 - Croatia 1
6.9.97	Croatia 3 - Bosnia 2
10.9.97	Denmark 3 - Croatia 1
11.10.97	Slovenia 1 - Croatia 3

Final Table

	P	W	D	L	F	A	Pts
Denmark	8	5	2	1	14	6	17
CROATIA	8	4	3	1	17	12	15
Greece	8	4	2	2	11	4	14
Bosnia	8	3	0	5	9	14	9
Slovenia	8	0	1	7	5	20	1

PLAY-OFFS

29.10.97	Croatia 2 - Ukraine 0
15.11.97	Ukraine 1 - Croatia 1

CROATIA FACT FILE

Colours: Red and white chequered shirts, white shorts, blue socks

Coach: Miroslav Blazevic

WORLD CUP FINALS RECORD

First time qualifiers this year

53

THE STORY *of the* WORLD CUP

1930   HOSTS: URUGUAY   CHAMPIONS: URUGUAY

The world's most prestigious soccer tournament was a long time in the making. The idea was initially suggested in 1904 at a meeting in Paris which also saw the foundation of FIFA, the governing body of world football. Twenty-six years later FIFA had 41 member countries, but just thirteen of them competed in the first World Cup finals: four from Europe, seven from South America, plus the USA and Mexico.

Uruguay, home of the then reigning Olympic soccer champions, was chosen to host the tournament. Uruguay showed their class and won through to the final against neighbouring Argentina. The match, played in Montevideo in front of 90,000 fans, was controlled by a referee who insisted that his life be insured before he took to the pitch! Argentina supplied the football used in the first 45 minutes, and Uruguay provided the second-half ball! By half-time Argentina were leading 2-1. At the end of 90 minutes Uruguay had turned the game around, to win 4-2 and earn themselves the distinction of becoming the very first World Cup holders.

1934   HOSTS: ITALY   CHAMPIONS: ITALY

Italy hosted the second World Cup finals. Thirty-two nations participated, but reigning champions Uruguay declined to enter in protest at the poor European turnout four years earlier. A qualifying tournament settled the sixteen finalists. En route to the last stage Italy won through a controversial replay with Spain in the second round, and beat favourites Austria in the semi-final. In the final on 10 June, Italy met Czechoslovakia in Rome. It was a hard-fought contest, in which Puc scored for the Czechs in the 70th minute. Twelve minutes later Orsi equalised for the hosts with a fluke shot that curled tantalisingly into the Czech net and took the game into extra time. Schiavio became a national hero, when he shot the only remaining goal for Italy.

1938   HOSTS: FRANCE   CHAMPIONS: ITALY

The third series, in 1938, was played in France amid an atmosphere of worsening political tension. Under coach Vittorio Pozzo the Italians eliminated the hosts in the second round, and went on to became the first nation to retain the World Cup. After beating Brazil in the semi-finals, they met Hungary in the final in Paris on 19 June. Two goals each from Colaussi and Piola gave Italy a 4-2 victory. This tournament was also notable for the emergence of Brazil as a footballing power. Their striker Leonidas da Silva was the most exciting player on display. Known as the 'Black Diamond', Leonidas was the tournament's leading scorer with eight goals. He was rested for the semi-final encounter, a decision later regarded as a monumental error.

1950   HOSTS: BRAZIL   CHAMPIONS: URUGUAY

The 1942 World Cup finals were to have been staged in either Argentina or Brazil. But the Second World War intervened and twelve years elapsed between the third and fourth series. By then the most prized trophy in world football was officially titled the Jules Rimet Trophy *(pictured left)*, in honour of one of FIFA's founding fathers. Brazil was chosen to host the 1950 finals. In celebration they built a brand new stadium, the fabulous Maracana in Rio de Janeiro, with a capacity of 200,000. For the first and only time the tournament was run entirely on a league basis, with the winners of four groups eventually playing for points in the final round. Brazil were hot favourites, and they duly won through to the last stage, along with Uruguay, Sweden and Spain.

In the end it all boiled down to the 'final' match – Brazil v Uruguay, attended by a record 199,854 fans in the Maracana on 16 July. The hosts needed only to draw to lift the World Cup, but they saw Uruguay claw back a 1-0 deficit in the second half to emerge as World Champions for the second time, with a 2-1 victory. England, making their first foray into World Cup football, started well with a 2-0 defeat of Chile. But they were then defeated 1-0 by the USA in the shock result of the tournament.

1927 1928 1929 **1930** 1931 1932 1933 **1934** 1935
1936 1937 **1938** 1939 1940 1941 1942 1943 1944
1945 1946 1947 1948 1949 **1950** 1951 1952 1953
1954 1955 1956 1957 **1958** 1959 1960 1961 **1962**
1963 1964 1965 **1966** 1967 1968 1969 **1970** 1971
1972 1973 **1974** 1975 1976 1977 **1978** 1979 1980
1981 **1982** 1983 1984 1985 **1986** 1987 1988 1989
1990 1991 1992 1993 **1994** 1995 1996 1997 **1998**

1954 HOSTS: SWITZERLAND   CHAMPIONS: WEST GERMANY

Hungary, the 'Magical Magyars', took the footballing world by storm in the early '50s. In '53, among other notable results, they had become the first non-British side to beat England at Wembley – and they did it with an emphatic 6-3 margin. Their star players Puskas, Czibor, Hidegkuti and Kocsis were names known all over the world. Such was their reputation as masters of the game, that by the time of the 1954 World Cup finals Hungary were firm favourites to become only the third nation to lift the trophy.

Hungary did reach the final, against West Germany, and within the first ten minutes they were two-up through goals from Puskas and Czibor. However, the Germans stuck to their task and gradually got back into the game.

With twelve minutes left, they had drawn level with goals from Morlock and Rahn. Then Rahn scored again to put West Germany ahead. Puskas found the net shortly afterwards, but the 'goal' was disallowed – and West Germany were World Champions for the first time.

1958 HOSTS: SWEDEN   CHAMPIONS: BRAZIL

The 1958 finals in Sweden produced two enduring legends. Frenchman Just Fontaine struck thirteen goals as his side marched to the semi-finals and eventually finished third. This remarkable individual scoring record has never been beaten, and probably never will be.

The other legend created in '58 was that of a Brazilian player of real flair and breathtaking skills. His name was Pelé, he was just 17 and he was destined to become the most famous footballer in the world. It was in Sweden that Brazil at last fulfilled their promise. En route to the final they topped their group, then beat Wales in the quarter-finals. In the semis they eliminated France with a 5-2 margin.

In the final, in Stockholm on 29 June, the brilliant Brazilians bamboozled host nation Sweden to win 5-2, and became the first nation to lift the World Cup outside their own continent. Pelé scored twice in the match. His first was a virtuoso goal that is still revered as one of the best ever scored in a World Cup final.

1962 HOSTS: CHILE   CHAMPIONS: BRAZIL

Despite an early injury to star player Pelé, the yellow-shirted wonders of Brazil marched on to the 1962 World Cup final in Santiago. Their opponents were Czechoslovakia, who were contesting their second World Cup final.

Masopust put the classy Czech side ahead in the 15th minute. Amarildo, Pelé's replacement, equalised for Brazil three minutes later. After that the reigning World Champions dominated the game to retain their crown as 3-1 victors. Their remaining goals came from Zito and Vava. The undoubted star of the 1962 tournament was Garrincha who, as a child had fought against physical difficulties, to emerge as a wonderful winger of breathtaking ability.

Pelé, arguably the greatest footballer of them all

THE STORY OF THE WORLD CUP

1966 HOSTS: ENGLAND   CHAMPIONS: ENGLAND

Brazil's good fortune was left high and dry in England in 1966. The reigning World Champions were eliminated in the opening round, following defeats by Hungary and Portugal. Another faller at this stage was Italy, beaten by North Korea in one of the shock results of the tournament and finding themselves unable to recover.

Meanwhile, the host nation – under the guidance of manager Alf Ramsey – progressed unbeaten from Group One. A fine theorist, Ramsey had been appointed England's coach in 1963, after insisting on complete control over team matters. He then predicted that his side would win the 1966 World Cup. His squad, centred on the talents of Bobby Moore, Bobby Charlton, Jimmy Greaves and Gordon Banks, was solid and dependable – and they took full advantage of their 'home' status.

After the Group stage England beat Argentina 1-0 in the quarter-finals, a match marred by the sending-off of Argentina's skipper Rattin. In the semi-finals England notched up a 2-1 victory over Portugal, whose team included Eusebio – one of the stars of the tournament and destined to finish as leading scorer with nine goals. Both English goals came from Bobby Charlton and they set the stage for the final encounter with West Germany, at Wembley on 30 July.

Goal-getter Greaves, injured early in the tournament, had been replaced by Geoff Hurst of West Ham. Hurst seized his chance and became the first player to score a hat-trick in a World Cup final. But it was West Germany who scored first, through Haller in the 13th minute. Hurst got England back on level terms six minutes later, and at half-time the game was finely balanced at 1-1. The scales were tipped in England's favour in the 78th minute when Martin Peters beat Tilkowski in the German goal. Then, in the last minute of normal time, Weber struck the equaliser and forced the game into extra time.

Inspired by Alf Ramsey's team talk, England's eleven lionhearts had but a single thought in mind – to regain the lead and hold on to it. In the 100th minute Geoff Hurst scored his second goal – in one of the most controversial moments in soccer history. Connecting with an Alan Ball cross, the striker hammered the ball against the underside of the crossbar. It thundered down onto the goal-line and the West Germans claimed that the ball had not entirely crossed the line. The referee consulted his linesman and then signalled that the goal stood. England had regained the initiative. Geoff Hurst rounded off the most memorable afternoon of his career by firing home a 20-yard shot to complete that famous hat-trick. 'Some people are on the pitch, they think it's all over...it is now!' yelled BBC TV commentator Kenneth Wolstenholme, setting the seal on English football's moment of crowning glory.

1970 HOSTS: MEXICO   CHAMPIONS: BRAZIL

When the World Cup competition was originally inaugurated, FIFA declared that any team who won the title three times would keep the trophy for ever – but they never expected such a thing to happen. By 1970 Brazil and Italy had that goal in mind. Both had won the World Cup twice, and both were determined to put the disappointment of 1966 behind them. Brazil's renowned flair for imaginative football swept them to the final, in Mexico City's Azteca Stadium on 21 June. Pelé, back to fitness and at the top of his form, was a prime factor in this achievement. Italy, a team constructed around a mean and magnificent defence, provided the opposition. It was a fascinating battle of wills, that seemed evenly poised. In the end, the brilliance of the Brazilians won the day. Pelé opened the scoring with a stunning header. Boninsegna equalised for Italy. But further goals from Gerson, Jairzinho and Carlos Alberto sealed the result at 4-1 in Brazil's favour and the Jules Rimet Trophy now belonged to them – for ever!

1974 HOSTS: WEST GERMANY   CHAMPIONS: WEST GERMANY

In 1974 the 'FIFA World Cup Trophy' was the new prize at the pinnacle of the world game. West Germany, inspired by skipper Franz Beckenbauer, reached the final in Munich's Olympic Stadium on 7 July. Their opponents were the orange-shirted, 'total football' machine of Holland, inspired by the world's top player Johan Cruyff. Before a West German player had so much as touched the ball, English referee Jack Taylor awarded a penalty to Holland when Cruyff was brought down. Neeskens put the Dutch team into the lead from the spot. Relentless pressure by the West Germans brought them back into the game – and goals from Brietner and Muller turned the scoreline around and made West Germany World Champions for the second time.

1978 HOSTS: ARGENTINA   CHAMPIONS: ARGENTINA

In 1978, Holland, without Johan Cruyff, made it to a second successive World Cup final. Once again the host nation provided the opposition – and once again Holland finished as runners-up. Played in Buenos Aires on 25 June, this World Cup final was a grim game, characterised by a string of stoppages and cynical fouls. Kempes opened the scoring for Argentina in the 38th minute. The hosts then proceeded to defend their lead and held out until the 82nd minute when Dutch substitute Nanninga equalised. Holland almost snatched victory, but Rensenbrink's last-minute effort rebounded agonisingly off the post. The game went to extra time and further goals from Kempes and Bertoni earned Argentina a 3-1 victory.

THE STORY OF THE WORLD CUP

1982 HOSTS: SPAIN

CHAMPIONS: ITALY

In 1982 the World Cup finals was contested for the first time by 24 finalists, and the time needed to complete the tournament was extended to almost a month. Host nation Spain failed to progress beyond the second Group stage, which provided the four semi-finalists — Italy, Poland, West Germany and France. Italy beat Poland 2-0 in Barcelona, while West Germany got through in a nail-biting penalty shoot-out against France in Seville after a 3-3 draw. The final, in Madrid, was an evenly-balanced encounter until Italy's inspiration, Paolo Rossi, broke the deadlock in the 56th minute. Further Italian goals came from Tardelli and Altobelli. West Germany replied through Breitner. But Italy were worthy of their 3-1 victory and became only the second nation to win the World Cup three times.

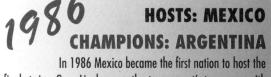

Paolo Rossi scores for Italy against West Germany in the 1982 World Cup Final

1986 HOSTS: MEXICO
CHAMPIONS: ARGENTINA

In 1986 Mexico became the first nation to host the finals twice. Gary Lineker was the tournament's top scorer with six goals, including a brilliant hat-trick against Poland which secured England's passage to the second round. A 3-0 defeat of Paraguay took England into the quarter-finals where they met Argentina. That match turned on arguably the most dubious refereeing decision in World Cup history — the notorious 'Hand of God' incident that led to Argentina's first goal when Diego Maradona's arm nudged the ball past Peter Shilton. The goal was given amid massed English protests. Maradona later added a wonderful solo goal, but it was his first that sticks in the memory, as England went down 2-1.

Argentina went on to the final against West Germany in the Azteca Stadium on 29 June. Brown and Valdano put the Argentinians 2-0 ahead, only to see West Germany claw their way back into the contest with goals from Rummenigge and Voller. The winner came from Burruchaga, who put the finishing touch on a wonderful pass from the man whose name will always be associated with the 1986 finals — Diego Maradona.

Diego Maradona with the World Cup in 1986

Maradona en route to scoring his second goal against England in the 1986 quarter-final

1990

HOSTS: ITALY
CHAMPIONS: WEST GERMANY

The fourteenth finals began with a real shock, when Cameroon defeated reigning champions Argentina in the opening game – a result that set the scene for a most entertaining tournament. Led by Bobby Robson, England reached the semi-finals but went out to West Germany in a penalty shoot-out. It was in this match that Paul Gascoigne shed a few tears following a booking that would have meant him missing the final had England got through. In the end the 1986 finalists met again in Rome on 8 July. This time Argentina had a reversal of fortunes, losing to the only goal of a rather dour match, an Andy Brehme penalty kick in the 84th minute. Now West Germany joined the elite of nations who had lifted the World Cup trophy three times.

Cameroon defeat Argentina in the opening match of Italia '90

West Germany, 1990 World Cup winners

A distraught Paul Gascoigne is led from the field by Terry Butcher after England's semi-final defeat by West Germany in 1990

Baresi of Italy and Romario of Brazil in the 1994 World Cup Final

1994

HOSTS: USA
CHAMPIONS: BRAZIL

The USA presented a marvellous tournament in nine venues across the States, with the final being played at the Rose Bowl in Los Angeles. After the stirring Opening Ceremony at Soldier Field in Chicago, Germany took on Bolivia in the opening match on 17 June. A month later the 24 entrants had been reduced to two – Italy and Brazil. Brazil had the upper hand throughout the final, but were unable to make the necessary breakthrough. The match went into extra time, which also passed goal-less. And so, for the first time, the destination of the World Cup was decided by a penalty shoot-out. Three of Italy's star performers missed their spot kicks to give the trophy and the World Championship to Brazil for a record fourth time.

WORLD CUP FINAL VICTORIES

Brazil	4	–	1958, 1962, 1970, 1994
Italy	3	–	1934, 1938, 1982
West Germany	3	–	1954, 1974, 1990
Uruguay	2	–	1930, 1950
Argentina	2	–	1978, 1986
England	1	–	1966

WORLD CUP FINALS

YEAR	RESULT	VENUE
1930	Uruguay 4, Argentina 2	Montevideo, Uruguay
1934	Italy 2, Czechoslovakia 1 (aet)	Rome, Italy
1938	Italy 4, Hungary 2	Paris, France
1950	Uruguay 2, Brazil 1	Rio de Janeiro, Brazil
1954	West Germany 3, Hungary 2	Berne, Switzerland
1958	Brazil 5, Sweden 2	Stockholm, Sweden
1962	Brazil 3, Czechoslovakia 1	Santiago, Chile
1966	England 4, West Germany 2 (aet)	London, England
1970	Brazil 4, Italy 1	Mexico City, Mexico
1974	West Germany 2, Holland 1	Munich, West Germany
1978	Argentina 3, Holland 1 (aet)	Buenos Aires, Argentina
1982	Italy 3, West Germany 1	Madrid, Spain
1986	Argentina 3, West Germany 2	Mexico City, Mexico
1990	West Germany 1, Argentina 0	Rome, Italy
1994	Brazil 0, Italy 0	Los Angeles, USA
	(Brazil won 3-2 on penalties)	

TOP SCORERS

1930	Stabile	Argentina	8
1934	Schiavio	Italy	4
	Nejedly	Czechoslovakia	4
	Conen	Germany	4
1938	Leonidas Da Silva	Brazil	8
1950	Ademir	Brazil	9
1954	Kocsis	Hungary	11
1958	Fontaine	France	13
1962	Jerkovic	Yugoslavia	5
1966	Eusebio	Portugal	9
1970	Muller	West Germany	10
1974	Lato	Poland	7
1978	Kempes	Argentina	6
1982	Rossi	Italy	6
1986	Lineker	England	6
1990	Schillaci	Italy	6
1994	Salenko	Russia	6
	Stoichkov	Bulgaria	6

TOTALLY 100%
WORLD
CUP 98
UNOFFICIAL

1998 WORLD CUP FINAL

Track the progress of the World Cup finals b

GROUP A

Wed 10 June	Saint-Denis	Brazil	__ v Scotland	__
Wed 10 June	Montpellier	Morocco	__ v Norway	__
Tue 16 June	Bordeaux	Scotland	__ v Norway	__
Tue 16 June	Nantes	Brazil	__ v Morocco	__
Tue 23 June	Marseille	Brazil	__ v Norway	__
Tue 23 June	Saint-Etienne	Scotland	__ v Morocco	__

Final Table

	P	W	D	L	F	A	Pts
1	3						
2	3						
3	3						
4	3						

GROUP B

Thu 11 June	Bordeaux	Italy	__ v Chile	__
Thu 11 June	Toulouse	Cameroon	__ v Austria	__
Wed 17 June	Saint-Etienne	Chile	__ v Austria	__
Wed 17 June	Montpellier	Italy	__ v Cameroon	__
Tue 23 June	Saint-Denis	Italy	__ v Austria	__
Tue 23 June	Nantes	Chile	__ v Cameroon	__

Final Table

	P	W	D	L	F	A	Pts
1	3						
2	3						
3	3						
4	3						

GROUP C

Fri 12 June	Lens	S Arabia	__ v Denmark	__
Fri 12 June	Marseille	France	__ v S Africa	__
Thu 18 June	Toulouse	S Africa	__ v Denmark	__
Thu 18 June	Saint-Denis	France	__ v S Arabia	__
Wed 24 June	Lyon	France	__ v Denmark	__
Wed 24 June	Bordeaux	S Africa	__ v S Arabia	__

Final Table

	P	W	D	L	F	A	Pts
1	3						
2	3						
3	3						
4	3						

GROUP D

Fri 12 June	Montpellier	Paraguay	__ v Bulgaria	__
Sat 13 June	Nantes	Spain	__ v Nigeria	__
Fri 19 June	Paris	Nigeria	__ v Bulgaria	__
Fri 19 June	Saint-Etienne	Spain	__ v Paraguay	__
Wed 24 June	Lens	Spain	__ v Bulgaria	__
Wed 24 June	Toulouse	Nigeria	__ v Paraguay	__

Final Table

	P	W	D	L	F	A	Pts
1	3						
2	3						
3	3						
4	3						

GROUP E

Sat 13 June	Lyon	S Korea	__ v Mexico	__
Sat 13 June	Saint-Denis	Holland	__ v Belgium	__
Sat 20 June	Bordeaux	Belgium	__ v Mexico	__
Sat 20 June	Marseille	Holland	__ v S Korea	__
Thu 25 June	Saint-Etienne	Holland	__ v Mexico	__
Thu 25 June	Paris	Belgium	__ v S Korea	__

Final Table

	P	W	D	L	F	A	Pts
1	3						
2	3						
3	3						
4	3						

GROUP F

Sun 14 June	Saint-Etienne	Yugoslavia	__ v Iran	__
Mon 15 June	Paris	Germany	__ v USA	__
Sun 21 June	Lens	Germany	__ v Yugoslavia	__
Sun 21 June	Lyon	USA	__ v Iran	__
Thu 25 June	Montpellier	Germany	__ v Iran	__
Thu 25 June	Nantes	USA	__ v Yugoslavia	__

Final Table

	P	W	D	L	F	A	Pts
1	3						
2	3						
3	3						
4	3						

GROUP G

Mon 15 June	Marseille	England	__ v Tunisia	__
Mon 15 June	Lyon	Romania	__ v Colombia	__
Mon 22 June	Montpellier	Colombia	__ v Tunisia	__
Mon 22 June	Toulouse	Romania	__ v England	__
Fri 26 June	Saint-Denis	Romania	__ v Tunisia	__
Fri 26 June	Lens	Colombia	__ v England	__

Final Table

	P	W	D	L	F	A	Pts
1	3						
2	3						
3	3						
4	3						

GROUP H

Sun 14 June	Toulouse	Argentina	__ v Japan	__
Sun 14 June	Lens	Jamaica	__ v Croatia	__
Sat 20 June	Nantes	Japan	__ v Croatia	__
Sun 21 June	Paris	Argentina	__ v Jamaica	__
Fri 26 June	Bordeaux	Argentina	__ v Croatia	__
Fri 26 June	Lyon	Japan	__ v Jamaica	__

Final Table

	P	W	D	L	F	A	Pts
1	3						
2	3						
3	3						
4	3						

60

NOW ENTER THE GROUP WINNERS AND RUNNERS-UP ON THE SECOND ROUND CHART

OUNTDOWN CHART

ompleting this chart as the tournament unfolds...

SECOND ROUND

ame 1	Sat 27 June	Paris	Group A Winners _____ __ v Group B Runners-up _____ __

ame 1   Sat 27 June   Paris   Group A Winners _____ __   v Group B Runners-up _____ __

ame 2   Sat 27 June   Marseille   Group B Winners _____ __   v Group A Runners-up _____ __

ame 3   Sun 28 June   Lens   Group C Winners _____ __   v Group D Runners-up _____ __

ame 4   Sun 28 June   Saint-Denis   Group D Winners _____ __   v Group C Runners-up _____ __

ame 5   Mon 29 June   Toulouse   Group E Winners _____ __   v Group F Runners-up _____ __

ame 6   Mon 29 June   Montpellier   Group F Winners _____ __   v Group E Runners-up _____ __

ame 7   Tue 30 June   Bordeaux   Group G Winners _____ __   v Group H Runners-up _____ __

ame 8   Tue 30 June   Saint-Etienne Group H Winners _____ __   v Group G Runners-up _____ __

QUARTER-FINALS

ame A   Fri 3 July   Nantes   Game 1 Winners _____ __   v Game 4 Winners _____ __

ame B   Fri 3 July   Saint-Denis   Game 2 Winners _____ __   v Game 3 Winners _____ __

ame C   Sat 4 July   Marseille   Game 5 Winners _____ __   v Game 8 Winners _____ __

ame D   Sat 4 July   Lyon   Game 6 Winners _____ __   v Game 7 Winners _____ __

SEMI-FINALS

irst Semi-Final   Tuesday 7 July   Marseille
ame A Winners _____ __   v   Game C Winners _____ __

econd Semi-Final   Wednesday 8 July   Saint-Denis
ame B Winners _____ __   v   Game D Winners _____ __

THIRD PLACE PLAY-OFF

aturday 11 July   Paris

emi-Finals Losers _____ __   v   _____ __

1998 WORLD CUP FINAL

unday 12 July   Saint-Denis

_____ __   v   _____ __

HE 1998 WORLD CHAMPIONS ARE:

TOURNAMENT TOP SCORERS

Player	Country	No. of Goals	Player	Country	No. of Goals
1.			4.		
2.			5.		
3.			6.		

61